Everyday Angels

Everyday Angels

Everyone has an angel to help them

Jenny Smedley

HAY HOUSE

HAY HOUSE

Australia • Canada • Hong Kong • India
South Africa • United Kingdom • United States

First published and distributed in the United Kingdom by:
Hay House UK Ltd, 292B Kensal Rd, London W10 5BE. Tel.: (44) 20 8962 1230;
Fax: (44) 20 8962 1239. www.hayhouse.co.uk

Published and distributed in the United States of America by:
Hay House, Inc., PO Box 5100, Carlsbad, CA 92018-5100. Tel.: (1) 760 431 7695
or (800) 654 5126; Fax: (1) 760 431 6948 or (800) 650 5115. www.hayhouse.com

Published and distributed in Australia by:
Hay House Australia Ltd, 18/36 Ralph St, Alexandria NSW 2015.
Tel.: (61) 2 9669 4299; Fax: (61) 2 9669 4144. www.hayhouse.com.au

Published and distributed in the Republic of South Africa by:
Hay House SA (Pty), Ltd, PO Box 990, Witkoppen 2068.
Tel./Fax: (27) 11 467 8904. www.hayhouse.co.za

Published and distributed in India by:
Hay House Publishers India, Muskaan Complex, Plot No.3, B-2, Vasant Kunj,
New Delhi – 110 070. Tel.: (91) 11 4176 1620; Fax: (91) 11 4176 1630.
www.hayhouse.co.in

Distributed in Canada by:
Raincoast, 9050 Shaughnessy St, Vancouver, BC V6P 6E5. Tel.: (1) 604 323 7100;
Fax: (1) 604 323 2600

© Jenny Smedley, 2010

A catalogue record for this book is available from the British Library.
ISBN 978-1-84850-204-8

Printed and bound in Great Britain by CPI Bookmarque, Croydon CR0 4TD.

This book is dedicated to my own personal angels in thanks for the gifts they have given me.

I also dedicate it to my soul mate and best friend, Tony, for all his support throughout my life.

I'd also like to thank all the hard workers at Hay House for making my books into realities.

CONTENTS

PREFACE

In every religion, every country and every culture, angels are recognized in some form or another as being messengers between humans and God. Their shapes are many and varied; one of the most interesting is found in Native American cultures, where angels are known as *Thunderbirds*, winged spirits in the form of giant birds who are said to bring messages and signs from the creator. However, angels can appear in any shape or form. I've had an angel appear as a golden column, a traditional winged being, and even once in the guise of an elderly lady looking for help. So, when seeking angels, expect the unexpected.

There have to be angels, for if all prayers and pleas for help went directly to God, well, then chaos might ensue. If God himself received every request for help with a parking space or even with healing for an ailing loved one, how could all the requests possibly be dealt with? Of course God, or any supreme being, would be omnipotent, all powerful, but what about the added complications when an act of compassion towards one person might create possible problems for another, or trigger a chain of events that might cause problems for the entire world? It makes sense to me that there are many dimensions that deal with many aspects of God and his helpers, the angels.

I believe angels are also something of an intermediary for communicating with God, necessary because it's very possible that connecting directly with God, by whatever means, could actually burn us out or damage us in some way, a bit like plugging your finger directly into the electricity mains!

Many people write to me and ask, 'Do I have an angel?' It makes me so sad when I read this, because I know that everyone has an angel of their own. In fact, each of us has several. It's upsetting to think that there are lonely people out there who feel that even the angels have deserted them, making them feel more alone than ever. Of course everyone has angels, but the difficulty is being able to connect with them and with all the other angels they could call upon for help, if they only knew how. My book *Angel Whispers* is a definitive manual on how to do just that, but still some people seem convinced that, although they believe that other people have angels, they don't think they themselves do, and that, therefore, there is little point in trying to make contact, because no angels will be there to hear them. They feel that somehow they don't deserve to have an angel.

The truth is that angels love us unconditionally, and will help us in any way they can, no matter what our status in the world. Angels have loved all members of the human race, from people like Mother Teresa all the way to Adolf Hitler. That is what 'unconditional' love means – to be loved no matter what our character or behaviour – and it's what we're privileged to receive from angels. So, this book was born to show you that *everyone*, no matter how humble, no matter how sad, no matter what age, no matter how poor, or rich, no matter what race or creed, has an angel, in fact many angels, that they can call on. Angels are great equalizers. They don't care if you're black or white, big or small, young or old, male or female, famous or not, lonely or not, good or bad. All of us are equal in their eyes, for they see past the frailty and inadequacy of human nature right through to the soul beneath.

Hopefully, after reading this book those who doubted they had an angel will go back to *Angel Whispers* with renewed hope, and quickly get on the right track to receive angelic help in their lives. For other readers who already trust that they know their angel, I've filled parts of this book with beautiful stories sent to me from around the world which demonstrate that we all have divine access. I've also brought in new tips on how to keep the communication going and develop it further with greater understanding.

Here are some important facts about angels that you must never forget. Repeat them to yourself on those dark nights of doubt:

- Everyone is equal in the eyes of angels.

- Angels will help everyone regardless of age, creed, colour or gender.

- Everyone is special in the eyes of angels.

- Positive thoughts bring positive angelic outcomes.

- Anyone can communicate with angels.

- Anyone can be helped by angels.

- Angels can appear in many shapes and forms, as naturally they are pure energy.

- There are different angels for different tasks.

- Some angels are easy to connect with – others take more dedication and effort than others.

- With angels, you get back what you put into the relationship.

- Angels love each of us unconditionally. No matter what we do, that never changes.

- A belief in angels helps a person to connect with them.

- Whatever your name is, whoever you are, *you* have an angel.

INTRODUCTION

Be not forgetful to entertain strangers, for thereby some have entertained angels unawares. – **Hebrews 13:2**

Angels have been around me since I was very small, although I wouldn't necessarily have called them 'angels' at the time. It was natural to me, as it is to most children, to accept miracles as part of everyday life. I didn't know the term 'spiritual', and wouldn't have understood it, but I know now that I was a very spiritual child. That is to say I was intuitively at one with the natural world around me. I didn't care a fig for posh clothes or toys. I never worried about whether my hair was brushed or my clothes were spotless. I didn't have expensive dolls or computers or electronic games. I played using my imagination, something which is often stifled in today's kids, to their disadvantage. I had everything I needed from nature. I played in the grass, in the flower beds and in my mind. A wooden street sign, about 2' 6" high, with a leg at each end, was my longed-for pony, and I would 'ride' it through the mists of my imaginary world for hours, a blanket and ropes fastened around it for a saddle and bridle. I was happy.

Playing this way, through imagination, is very akin to meditating. Children who play in this way are very switched off to the matters of the real world, and very open, therefore, to matters of the spiritual world, and to angels. In many cases, today's children have the work of the imagination provided for them by computer games and are not so fortunate. They have to work much harder to be happy because they're taught to focus on the material above all else. I think it's very important for the world that our future citizens become aware of the spirituality around them and become reconnected to the natural world. Apart from the obvious drawbacks of raising a generation that cares mostly about designer labels and the next big electronic craze, there's also the point that connecting with angels is all about energy. If your energy is the right kind, then raising it enough to commune with angels is very possible. Unfortunately electronic devices create precisely the wrong kind of energy. The fact that we bombard our children with this sort of energy from mobile phone masts, WI-FI and TV and radio signals is a great worry to me, as I feel it should be for everyone. Children who are ripped away from angelic connections will have a strong tendency to become greedy, grasping and, despite all their material possessions, desperately unfulfilled and unhappy as adults. That would be bad for all of us.

Of course as I grew up, things changed for me, too. I was changed, by life, by being human, by other people, by a need to fit in socially with my peers. Like all children I was moulded by well-meaning grown-ups, who only wanted me to fit into society, but in doing so they inadvertently stifled my individuality. Later in life when I wanted to find myself and my angels again, it took me many years to get back to the place where I regained that connection, but at last I managed it and was brought out of depression and into a fulfilled life. I had been brought very low by then, and being brought out of it not only intact but 100 per cent better than ever before was a real testament to the power of angels.

I continue to this day to get wonderful help from my angels. Once I had been shown my role in life, to be a spiritual seed-planter in people, I was given several tools. One of these was a TV show that ran for two years, enabling me to learn from all my guests – hundreds of spiritual teachers and people who'd had amazing angelic encounters. I was given the ability to create remote aura pictures from ordinary photographs, and digitally paint angel portraits. I was also given psychic ability, which all enabled me to be commissioned to write magazine columns, in order to reach more people and plant seeds of spirituality in them. I gained an amazing friend who helped me promote what I do, allowing me to partake in over 400 radio interviews over the years.

ANGEL SURPRISES

Angels have always been able to surprise me, and nowadays they still do. Just when I think they've helped me to help others as much as they can, they come up with something new and even more amazing. I have often been woken in the night by angels giving me messages, so I've learned to keep a pen and paper beside the bed to take notes. It's an essential thing for anyone trying to communicate with angels. However much you think you're going to recall something, quite often the mists of sleep cloud your memory. More than once I've woken in the morning knowing that in the night I was told something incredible, and I can almost still grasp it, only to have it fade as fast as sand through my fingers. It's very frustrating, because in the night, in semi-sleep, I'll have been thinking, *that's amazing! It explains everything! It's all so simple,* and I've been totally certain that the news was so incredible that I couldn't possibly forget it, but I did. Perhaps I was meant to, but now I keep notes – even though sometimes I'm so sleepy that I can't even open my eyes, I feel for the pad and pen in the darkness and scribble as best I can.

In my work I came to realize that most of what I was doing involved helping people in distress as well as seed-planting among the curious. The best way to do this was to help them connect with their own angels, which is why Hay House had me write *Angel Whispers – how to get closer to your angel,* as it's always better and more effective to communicate directly with the angels than to do so through another person, and that has worked very well for a lot of people.

The angels are also aware, however, that some people are just too distressed to be able to follow instructions or persevere enough to get through to the angelic realms. Sometimes their circumstances are so dire that they can't see a way to be positive even for a second. You can liken it to their energy being a small boat on an ocean. The angels, and the help they could deliver, are a raft trying to reach the person and their 'boat'. But no matter how much they want the angels' help, if the person's energy is so fragmented and unbalanced that it makes the 'sea' around the person rough, they are actually pushing their angel's 'raft' away. If they can control their energy and make the sea around the boat calm, then the raft can reach them. In the depths of pain, despair or darkness, people are unable to smooth out their energy. It can become a downward spiral they can't escape from.

ANGEL STAR

So, on this particular night I was woken to something rather special, which was a tool to help these people with my own angel-inspired energy. I woke up and realized that there was something sparkling in the air above my head. This was very odd, because the bedroom was actually in total darkness – there was nothing there to provide reflected or actual light, and yet there it was. I looked up and saw the most beautiful star-shaped crystal floating in the darkness. It wasn't like a Christmas tree star, with just five points: this had multiple points, and reminded me of something that might have been at home on that beautiful, scintillating spaceship in the *Close Encounters* movie.

The star also shone and flickered with rainbow colours that flashed off the points as the star slowly turned in the air. I knew it was an angel star.

After I while I realized what I had to do, and I reached up to grasp it. As soon as my hand closed around it, the visual impression vanished, but the star hadn't gone. I could feel it pulsing gently in my hand, even though I couldn't see it. As I settled back down, cradling the star against me in my hand, I started to be told what these magical objects were for. I heard that I'd be able to transfer one, as energy, through the quantum universe (where everything and everyone is pure energy) to people who needed help and were judged by the angels to be in the right place and in the right time to receive help. I'd be able to enter the person's energy field on a quantum level, as I do when I am doing readings for them, and hand them over the angel star, which they would then be able to hold, even though they'd never see it. The star would transfer its angel power to them when the need arose.

The next morning I was quite excited to see this new tool in action, and just as I expected I got an email almost immediately from someone who needed the help of the angel star crystal. This woman, Lynn, was petrified at the thought of her approaching back surgery. She was convinced she'd die under the anaesthetic, or not recover well and be crippled for life. Her problem was caused by a bony spur growing on her spine. I wrote back to her and told her about the star. I told her she could expect to receive it momentarily and that it would help calm her. She wrote back ecstatically, feeling the energy immediately, and over the next few days, any time she panicked she would open her hand and feel the star alight there. She would be calm immediately. What neither of us expected, though, was that within a few days her pain had eased so much that she was able to go shopping for the first time in months, and wondered if she still needed surgery. Of course I told her she must talk to her doctor before making any decisions. When she was examined it seemed that the spur had partially broken off and so her pain had lessened. However, she would still have some surgery to prevent the condition recurring. The operation would be much less traumatic, though, because she had total faith in the star protecting her and, as it had already vastly improved her condition, she knew it would go on to help her make a full recovery.

I then got an email from a mum who was terribly concerned about her daughter. This young woman was carrying dark energy with her which was making her have suicidal thoughts. The girl felt alone and unloved. Immediately she got her star, she started to feel better about herself, and went on to make new friends because people saw her differently. It seemed the star had removed the dark energy that had been making people keep her at arm's length.

I recently did a mini-workshop at the Cardiff Natural Health Show; afterwards I was able to dispense over 20 angel stars to members of the audience. It's extraordinary that, with no prior knowledge of an individual's problems, every star came complete to me with a message that was very meaningful for the person concerned. The colours and shapes also varied, depending on what the star was for. It made a long day very worthwhile to see the joy in their faces as each and every one of them felt their star touch down into their open hands.

Another problem people sometimes have is that their self-esteem is so low that they really can't believe they have any angels, and one woman actually wrote to me and said she thought her angels hated her! Both of these things are impossible. Everyone has an angel, every soul is capable of connecting to angels, and angels are incapable of hating their charges! I'm sure they sometimes might find us frustrating, but they could never hate us.

In reading the personal accounts and chapters that follow I hope that every single one of you will come to understand that there are angels out there for every purpose you can possibly imagine, and a lot that you can't, and, most importantly, there are angels out there for *you!*

CHAPTER 1

ANGELS ARE EVERYWHERE

The key to a happy life is to see angels everywhere.
– Jenny Smedley

We may all be familiar with the idea that praying to angels is a way to communicate with God, but what we can sometimes fail to spot are the messages from God to us! Angels bring us these messages, and they make their presence felt in a huge variety of ways. You might find a white feather fluttering to your feet, which wouldn't be unusual if you are walking next to a hedge, but if it happens in the middle of a supermarket, it could be from a different kind of 'bird' altogether!

Another classic is scent when there should be none, most predominately the perfume of a rose. Whenever my angel brings the presence of my mum through to me, she's always accompanied by the scent of freesias, which were my mum's favourite flowers.

More unexpectedly, perhaps, you might smell tobacco – a smoking angel? This won't really be tobacco, but the smell of burning white sage, a Native American cleansing herb.

Angels sometimes brush your cheek, with a touch as gentle as a cobweb. Sometimes there will be a gentle breeze when all the windows are shut. Sometimes you'll just have a feeling of total calm and safety.

People who are dying and have family with them have been heard to say that there are bright beings in the room who have come to collect them. While this might be disturbing for their relatives, the smile on the face of their dying loved one also fills them with joy and hope.

I recently received this question from a reader of my 'Angel Whisperer' column: 'Whenever my husband and I are out and about we see a white butterfly. What does it mean?'

This was my reply:

Butterflies are always a sign of renewal and regeneration, because they've recently emerged from a chrysalis, and before that they were a bit of a creepy-crawler caterpillar. They emerge into incredible beauty. White always means purity of heart. These signs from your angels recognize that you and your husband have been through some difficult times, and you've both had to be strong. Family difficulties and financial issues have plagued you, putting a damper on your happiness. These signs are also telling me that those hard times are over now, and the purity of your love is going to be able to shine through. When and if the butterflies stop com-

*ing to you, the time of abundance will revert to normality,
so make the very most of this time, because during it you
have no boundaries and nothing can stop you.*

THE BUTTERFLY CONNECTION

A woman called Mary-Ellen sent me a story that offers
another example of the 'butterfly connection' with angels:

*'My granddaddy and I grew very close in his latter years. I
didn't have parents by then, and I was happy that Granddaddy approved of my soon-to-be husband, Josh. He became more like a dad than a grandparent.*

*'It was in the build-up to our wedding that Granddaddy
became very ill, quite suddenly with pancreatic cancer. He
was given only weeks to live and it was a terrible shock. I
felt that I was going to have no family. He died the day
before the wedding, and both me and Josh were there to say
goodbye. It was very sad. My granddaddy made my fiancé
promise he'd always be there for me, and he did.*

*'The wedding took place in November in Canada, so it
was pretty cold. There was snow on the ground. In the middle of the ceremony a large blue butterfly appeared above
us where we stood, and then it landed on my left hand. Incredibly it stayed there, and none of us made any attempt to
move it, while Josh placed the wedding band on my finger.
As the words ending the ceremony were spoken the butterfly
took off and circled above us. It accompanied us to sign the
register, too. Everyone saw it. There shouldn't have been any*

butterflies around at that time. As we and the congregation started filing out for photos, the butterfly flew over us. I was getting a bit upset, as I felt drawn to it, and figured there was no way it would survive outside in the cold, and that even if it stayed in the church there was nothing for it to live on, so it was doomed. The photos done, I was looking up, watching it, wondering where it would go, when suddenly it just faded away. I swear, it didn't fly off, it just vanished. I couldn't believe it.

'It was later I wondered if my angel could have used the butterfly to let me know that Granddaddy was still close and watching over me. All I can say is that ever since then, whenever I ask for help, a blue butterfly will appear. Sometimes it's a real, live one, and sometimes it takes the form of a window hanging or an ornament in a store window, or even a logo on some packaging, but it's always there, somewhere.'

In this case the butterfly was certainly symbolizing that death is actually just a transition between this state of being and the next one, which will of course be infinitely more beautiful. Mary-Ellen's granddaddy had certainly been transmuted into a wonderful form.

ONLY CONNECT …

Another reader had this question: 'What sort of signs do my angels send me to tell me they're close? I often think I feel them, but if they had a special sign then I'd know for sure.'

This was my answer:

Your angels have quite an unusual sign to herald their presence: They fan you with their wings. So, next time you feel a gentle breeze wafting over your face when there shouldn't be one, you'll know for sure. This could happen indoors, or outside on a very calm day when there's no natural wind.

There is an endless variety of ways that your angel can choose to connect. The key to recognizing them is to notice unusual occurrences or coincidences. This was another question I received about another very unusual manifestation:

'I keep seeing donkeys! The other day I had just written in my diary, "I haven't seen them for donkey's years," referring to some friends, and suddenly I heard donkeys braying. I looked out of the window and two donkeys were being led into the museum opposite! A bit unnerved, I sat down to have a cuppa, opened a magazine and – a picture of a donkey looked up at me! Later I was driving down the motorway and suddenly realized I was following a truck with a sign on the back saying "Donkeys on board!" Perhaps they're trying to tell me something? I'm under a lot of stress at the moment and wondered if they were a sign of my "heavy load". If so, I wish they'd come and take some off me ...'

This was my answer:

You've been working very hard for some time and will continue to do so, most likely in caring for others. However, a helper is on the way. Someone who'll be of great service to you. This is what the signs are saying – so don't give up! Also make sure you accept and take advantage of the help that's coming, and don't be too proud to accept it! This helper will lift your overburdened spirit!

MOTORBIKE MESSAGE

I've already mentioned the myriad ways that angels can make their presence known, but I was recently sent a letter and a photograph that showed me another sign I'd never seen before. A man in Australia wrote to me by email to tell me that, after his partner had died in a terrible car crash, he was cleaning her motorbike in preparation for riding it to her funeral. He sprayed de-greaser on the motor and then left the cleaner on the bike for about 30 minutes so that it would have time to work. When he came back there were two perfectly shaped, linked pink love hearts formed beneath the bike where the cleaner had dripped on the driveway. There was no other drop of de-greaser left, except for a smiley mouth under the two hearts. The photograph was astounding to see.

So, look for the strangeness!

SYNCHRONICITY

These apparently meaningless 'coincidences' are really no such thing. They are synchronicity. What does that mean? It means the experience of two or more events that are seemingly unrelated and yet occur together in a way that gives them new meaning. If, for instance, you suddenly bump into an old friend, colleague or business acquaintance you haven't seen for a while, the chances are that it means something, especially if that person was inexplicably in your thoughts for a time before the meeting happened. When you do meet, either they will tell you something you need to know, introduce you to someone you need to meet, or possibly even change your life themselves with what may appear to be a casual word or random reference – so pay heed to everything they have to say. If you are about to call an old friend and they call you while you're thinking about them, listen very closely, because your guardian angel is trying to tell you something you need to know.

Supposing you've had a song in your head all day and your partner walks into the house singing the same song, or you both burst into the same song at the same time. Have a good look at the lyrics, because they may have a message for you. Pay attention to things that could be dismissed as meaningless coincidences, because there is no such thing, and anything that looks meaningless has been placed there by the mystical power that is synchronicity.

Follow the signs. Supposing you're driving down the road thinking about making a new business deal, and you're not sure if it's a good idea or not. Suddenly you notice that the car in front of you has a number plate that

reads BIG 123D. This could be interpreted as 'Big …
Deal – it's as easy as 1, 2, 3' – what's important is what it
might mean for *you*. And the thing about synchronistic
signs is that they nearly always come in threes, so later in
the day you might see a hoarding sign that you'd never
noticed before, that reads 'Today's the day to take a
chance …' Later still you might see a newspaper heading
that says, '2,000 new businesses forecast this year.' All
of these things could just be ignored, but a follower of
synchronicity will smile and say 'thank you,' and they'll
push forward with their business deal.

SIGNS ALL AROUND YOU

Angel signs increase exponentially, and this is a good
thing. The more you see the signs, the more you will
see the signs, and if you follow them, then before you
know it you'll be living a life that makes perfect sense,
instead of the meaningless, chaotic jumble most people
experience. You know when you buy a new car – a make
and colour that you've never had before? It's not one that
you've often seen, and you have probably been attracted
to it because it is a bit unusual – to you, that is. But once
you're driving around in it, you suddenly start to see more
and more cars that are the same. Is it that there are suddenly more of these vehicles, and that a whole bunch of
people suddenly made the same choice you did? No, it's
not that. Those cars were *always* there, it's just that your
brain and vision have become attuned to that car and that

colour, like never before, so you notice them now. They were always around, but you just didn't have any reason to notice them before. It's the same with angels. They have always been around, always there, always influencing us and trying to help us; you just didn't notice. The way to see them and notice them is to attune your brain and your energy to them.

'ODD-JOB ANGELS'

The easiest angels to get a handle on and to start to notice and use are what I call 'odd-job' angels. These are the little angel 'energy balls' that can help with everyday events such as changing the energy to help you in selling your house, finding you a parking space or finding something you've mislaid.

My friend of many years was trying very hard to sell her house. She and her husband were in the middle of a messy divorce. Neither of them could afford to move out of their charming little cottage, so until they could sell they were stuck rubbing shoulders with each other. It was a very uncomfortable situation. This all made for a lot of negative energy, and things got worse: first there were no offers, then not even any viewings! Of course would-be buyers were sensing all the negative energy in the house and, as this energy grew, even the photo of the house seen in the estate agent's window would turn people off.

I was able to tune in to some little odd-jobbers in the house (they are everywhere!) and discover what was needed. The house had to have a good cleansing with some sage smudging; that would help somewhat with the impressions the photos were giving, and therefore bring some viewings. To prepare for them I then helped my friend into a meditation with the odd-jobbers herself (it's always best to go direct!) and told her how to ask, sweetly and simply, for their help in selling the house. She did very well and felt that the angels wanted to vibrate to the colour blue, so she painted the once red front door blue, bought some blue tumble stones and placed them around the house, and finally put a very lovely blue labradorite crystal under the doormat so that every viewer had to walk over it. This stone would take away any sense of negative energy as they passed over it and give them a feeling of 'home'. (More about angels and colours later on.)

Within a week she had not one but two potential buyers and was able to choose the one in the best position for the quickest sale and resolution to her and her ex-husband's worries.

PARKING PROBLEMS AND LOST PROPERTY
Car-parking angels are legendary. This story came to me from a reader called Sarah:

'I'd been driving around Salisbury town for ages looking for somewhere to park that didn't entail me walking miles with my shopping, but I was having no luck. It was 23rd December 2008, so it wasn't really surprising that all the

world and his friend were trying to do the same thing! There were several incidences of 'parking rage' going on as drivers thought that someone else had nicked their space at the last minute. I was really on the verge of giving up and going home empty-handed. A vision of that ad on the TV where the man ends up buying all his relatives things like new windscreen-wiper rubbers for Christmas was the only thing that stopped me.

'There was one gift shop in particular that I wanted to get to, but how? Then I recalled hearing Jenny talking on the local radio and mentioning how "parking angels" could help if you really asked them and believed in them. I thought, "Why not? I don't have anything to lose." So I pictured the forecourt of the particular shop I wanted to go to. I was several streets away at that point. I pictured the shop very clearly with an empty space in the middle of the woefully small parking area at the front, and believed it would be there as much as was humanly possible. In my head I asked clearly for that slot to be vacant when I got there. I turned the final corner and, to my disappointment, saw that all the slots were filled. I almost despaired, but there was hope as no other cars were waiting. Then to my utter astonishment I saw the centre car's reversing lights go on and he backed out right in front of me. All I had to do was pull in. It was a real eye-opener for me! I never doubted again!'

Jane told me this little anecdote about the 'lost property angel':

'Of all the places to lose a gold necklace, a field of freshly cut hay has to be one of the worst. Not a needle in a haystack, but pretty close! I'd known the catch on the locket, which had once belonged to my mum, was a bit dodgy, but I felt so close to it that I guess I never thought I'd actually lose it. It was almost part of me. Besides, I felt naked without it and so I didn't want to leave it at home. Now I wished I had. I'd been helping a friend and fellow 'horse nut' cut her field of hay. It had been great fun. We'd all taken turns on the tractor and the dogs had rushed around all day like maniacs, chasing (but not catching) all the mice and rabbits that had fled the grass as it toppled into rows on the ground. We were all exhausted, all looking forward to a sit-down in front of my friend's Aga and a nice cup of tea, or glass of wine if we were lucky. We'd been about to walk back to the welcoming farmhouse when I realized my locket was gone. It was all I could do not to just break down and cry. I was tired, and now I was also very upset. Through my mind ran thoughts of getting metal detectors to come and scan the field, or gold dowsers, or something, because I couldn't imagine ever finding the thin gold chain and the rose gold locket strung on it in all this hay.

'My friend is very big on angels and it was her idea that we should ask for help and then walk up and down the field seeking guidance as to where the locket was lying. I felt a bit silly, but my friend closed her eyes and asked for help. We set off, me a little sceptical still, idly walking along, eyes glued to the ground, looking for a telltale twinkle of gold *from the too-fast setting sun. It was hopeless, wasn't it? On top of the fact that we had ten acres to search, it was also growing dark, slowly but surely. It was literally only maybe half a minute before my friend called to me from her side of the field. "Is this what you're looking for?" her smiling voice asked. I couldn't believe it – she'd virtually walked straight to it. A coincidence? Possibly, but I don't think so!'*

How would your day go, if the angels were working for you?

ANGELS ON YOUR RADAR

If you have the angels on your radar, then they will have you on theirs and things will just slide into place a little more easily for you throughout your day. You won't stub your toe in the bathroom, you won't burn the toast or row with your hubby over the morning paper, your kids will be quiet and listen, you won't have trouble parking the car or be late for the train, or have to sit next to someone with less than perfect hygiene and a penchant for listening to heavy metal on their iPod on the tube. I'm sure you're getting the idea by now. It won't be that there are absolutely no hitches for you, but any that there are won't affect your equilibrium or your general smooth progression through the day.

If you're not attuned to angels in any way, and they're not attuned to your energy, all of the above could easily go in reverse.

If the odd-job angels, or any angels, aren't helping you, how do you persuade them to?

First of all, as with all attempts at angel communication, you must calm your energy. I've said many times, but can't say it enough, that angels can't get through too much turbulent, negative energy, because that kind of energy vibrates in the lower dimensions and they can't go that low.

It's been discovered that there are around 35 dimensions, and although each one can be separated from the next by the width of a sheet of paper, vibrationally they are worlds away. It's said that God would exist at around level 35, angels of the sort we need to communicate with at around dimension 11, while we in our natural human form are at a lowly number 4. Angels need smooth positive energy to be able to pass through into our dimension, and even if we manage to raise our vibrational level, they still need to meet us half-way. Imagine you're a little plane bouncing along through turbulent air, and your angel is a refuelling plane trying to top you up. Unless you can reach calm air and fly on a level heading, the refuelling rig won't be able to hitch up to you. That's just how it is with you and angels. So, the best way to calm your energy is with a little meditation. Shut out all your worries and concentrate on breathing. Try not to doubt, because doubt is negative. When Peter Pan said that a fairy dies every time a child says she doesn't believe in them, he could almost have been talking about angels. They don't die, of course, but they become unavailable to us. It's much better for them and allows them to wield more power in our dimension if we believe in them and the help they can bring us.

Once you feel you're in the right frame of soul, ask for what you want, simply and with trust that you'll be answered. Don't try to conjure up complicated scenarios in which your wishes will be granted. Leave the 'hows' and 'whens' up to them. When things do start to go better for you, no matter how small the changes, then remember to say thank you! Believe that it was angel grace that helped you, and they will help you again. Grab on to the small things, hold them close, and like brooded eggs they'll hatch into bigger and better help and angel signs. Of course that works in reverse, too – if you hang on to the bad stuff, little problems will grow into bigger ones.

Suppose, for instance, you want to buy a new home and you're having trouble making what feels like the right decision from among several properties. If you build this up into a big problem in your mind, you'll be nurturing it, and the one decision that pops up at you and seems by its very prominence to be the right decision, will almost always be the wrong one. So, tell your angels what you want to know and ask them for a sign as guidance, and then just be calm and wait. Some sign will appear leading you to the right property.

When we first moved to Somerset from our farmhouse in Norfolk, we really weren't sure what we wanted. All we knew was that we wanted to get out of our rented property, which we hated, into a new home of our own. One of the houses we'd looked at was called 'Poppins'. After asking the angels for help, we were strolling through a nearby town, exploring and looking for somewhere to sit and have a cup of tea. We came across a café called 'Poppins'. Clear enough, and it was a very happy home indeed. When, six years later, we wanted to move back to town and came across a house called 'Pippins', it was more than a coincidence!

Supposing you want a new car and are afraid you'll end up with a 'lemon'. Ask your angels to guide you to the right vehicle. They will give you a natural aversion to certain colours, and that will help you to intuitively cut down on the myriad options. Then ask for a sign. The most common one you'll get in these cases is in the number plates. I was very drawn to our current car because of the message I perceived in the number plate.

These methods can work with any choices: jobs, partners, holiday destinations, etc. The clues are always in the clues!

CHAPTER 2
GUARDIAN ANGELS

The golden moments in the stream of life rush past us and we see nothing but sand; the angels come to visit us, and we only know them when they are gone. – **George Eliot**

Every single soul has an angel that's assigned to watch over it right from the moment of birth to the moment of death. There are no omissions and no one ever gets abandoned or left out. Guardian angels can intervene if we take a misstep, but ultimately we do have a path to walk, and they are therefore unable to change our fate completely. They can, however, make the journey we are destined to walk as smooth as possible. They can make our everyday lives as full with pleasure as possible, and nurture and nurse us through the tough times, lending us their strength. Guardian angels can also sometimes 'bring through' a loved one who has passed over, to reassure us that we never really die and are never really alone in the universe. They can bring us healing and pain relief in times of illness, and save us from accidents and mishaps that aren't necessary to our progress.

GUARDIAN ANGELS BRING US MESSAGES

Liz told me this lovely story:

'Many years ago when I was 13 (well, I did say many years ago), my younger brother died of leukaemia when he was 5 years old. For many years thereafter I kept having this dream in which I was passing the cemetery where he was buried, and I heard him call my name. I could see him clear as day, standing there, and I ran into the cemetery to get him and take him home. I could actually feel him and touch him, and I felt his tears on my face. He kept saying he wanted to go and see his grandpa, and I said I would take him. At that point in the dream a being of white would appear in front of me, and as I was very young I would always feel scared, but not scared, if you know what I mean. However, the person/angel would tell my wee brother that it was not possible for him to return to us, but he could visit for a wee while and I was allowed to take him. I would take him to my grandparents' home and he was welcomed with open arms, and then he would play happily with his toys. Then a loud knock would come at the door and he'd turn and tell me he had to go, and I'd try to stop him, but then I'd wake up.

'I kept getting this "dream", and often tried to stop myself from going into it but could not. This happened continually for about two years. The dream then stopped quite suddenly. I always believed the being in white was an angel who brought my brother to me. The strangest part of the dream was that, many years later, I still had told no one about it.

My parents were separated and my father was moving to England, and before he moved away he told a family friend that he had been having a strange dream for years. Guess what?! Same dream, although different house, and of course my dad was with my brother, not me, but apart from that the dream was identical. Do you think it was an angel or was I astral dreaming?'

My answer to Liz was that dreams that are repetitive like this are too deliberate to be just dreams, and the fact that her father was shown the exact same scenario tells me this was a real gift from the angels.

Shirley sent me this lovely story of how a guardian angel might bring comfort to the bereaved:

'I was 11 years old when my father died, and I had little understanding of what was happening to him at the time. I know now that he had bowel cancer and suffered terribly, my mother nursing him to the end.

'Around this time, I recall two occasions when I was lying on my bed, my mother having tucked me in for the night. Both times I glanced to the wall beside me and I was aware of a huge yellow pulsating light beamed onto the wall. I looked around the room to see where it was coming from but couldn't identify the source. I wasn't frightened, but I was bewildered, so the second time it happened I asked my mother what it was, as she was still in the room with me at the time. She had no idea what I was talking about,

and although I was pointing to the light and showing her where it was, she couldn't see it, so it appeared to be for my eyes only!

'It was really only in later years that I began to ponder on the experience. Was it my father coming to say goodbye, or was it an angel watching over me? I'd love to know which.'

I believe this was Shirley's angel bringing her a sign from her father, in the hopes that his death might give her hope further down the line in her life, rather than allowing her to despair too deeply at his loss at the time.

Lynda experienced another way angels have to make loved ones known to us:

'My grandmother (mum's mother) passed away in Jan 2005. Since her passing I've experienced rock crystals being thrown at me and landing at my feet, a shampoo bottle spinning, and even my iPod coming on by itself. I'm not worried about these things happening as I believe it's my angel sending me signs from my grandmother.'

Sharon recalled this story from her childhood.

'My little brother, William, had an experience none of us could ever explain, when he was about 2 years old. I've been taught that children have a natural close connection to angels. I've also been told that there are angels that will play with children sometimes, and bring through passed-

over loved ones for a visit, but I never thought it would happen to one of my family. Willy, as I called him then, wasn't very well. He was a bit grizzly, and as I had to sleep in the same room as him I was a bit grumpy about it. Being an older sister wasn't all it was cracked up to be as far as I was concerned then, but after this incident I started to see him in a different light! He had his cot filled with toys and yet he was demanding his "Polo Bear", which was all the way on the other side of the room. He called it "Polo Bear" because it was white and wore a woolly hat and scarf. He couldn't say "polar". He couldn't get it because at the time he still had the sides of his cot up at night. As well as being tired, I was feeling a bit sad, as our great-granny had just died. Willy had never met her as she lived in France, but I had, just once. Her house had a pool and I'd been hoping to go there again. I thought Willy was being a cry-baby, when really, people had died! I was a bit of a prima donna, I think. I was all of 7 years old at the time, and thought I was grown-up.

'Anyway, I told Willy to be glad he was alive and to go to sleep. A stupid thing to say to a 2-year-old, I know. Anyway, eventually he did go to sleep, and in the morning I was totally staggered to see he was cuddling Polo Bear. Then I realized, of course Mum must have come to check on him and given it to him. But he'd been asleep, I was sure, so how would she know he wanted it? When Willy woke up I asked him if Mummy had given Polo to him. "No," he said, "Ganmar came." I was sure he'd never known that's what

Mum had called Great-granny. She had done since she was a child. When Mum showed Willy a photo of Ganmar which she kept tucked away in her dressing table drawer, Willy said that was the lady who gave him Polo Bear.'

It's interesting that this angel was able to bring a kind of message through from Ganmar, but only to a child who'd never met her. It underlines that children are still connected to their spiritual selves, and are more receptive to messages than most adults are.

ANGELS THAT HEAL OR BRING RELIEF
This story comes from Chanelle:

'I had an accident recently and had been feeling sad because of it. In the accident I fractured my front tooth quite badly and broke the tooth next to it. Part of the fractured tooth has since been removed, but the gum area has been a little swollen – although apparently this is normal. I'd been feeling sad because of the accident, all the treatment and the mounting costs, because I'm a student at the moment. So balancing university work, the upset of the accident itself and money did get me upset sometimes. Anyway, I decided to really focus upon calling upon God and my angels to help me with the healing process (I needed the gum area to heal and the whole affected mouth area to heal so they could continue with the treatment and not have to do anything yucky – I'll spare you the gruesome details!).

'I felt that it was working, as I hadn't been experiencing the amount of pain that I thought I would, and that would normally be expected. Also, at one point during the treatment the anaesthetic had not kicked in, or had worn off a bit, so I felt some pain, but something told me to breathe slowly and relax. I did this and the pain went away.

'But I really called upon God and my angels one night, and had the following experience, though I can't explain what it was.

'I prayed to God and angels to heal my gum and affected mouth and teeth area, as well as continuing to guide me through the situation and give me strength – I also gave thanks for their assistance thus far.

'In the middle of the night I awoke and felt as if my head was being lifted off my pillow up to my bedroom ceiling. It was kind of misty and felt as if I was looking in on myself, really. I felt someone was putting my tooth back in, having taken it out. I felt a twinge of pain but then nothing. My gum area behind the worst affected tooth felt a bit puffy. I woke up and felt fine, and remembered the experience. I thought maybe it was God and the angels beginning the healing process. I said to them that if this was the case, thank you and to please give me a sign.

'I eventually fell back to sleep clutching my clear quartz and rose quartz crystals – I had these in my hand all along anyway. I then had a dream where I was visited by the Archangel Michael, with various messages, mostly to do with my father who I do not speak to due to incidents in *my childhood. One of these incidents has come back to me a lot since my accident actually, and I have been asking if it's time for me to stand in power and speak to my father about what happened and get some peace here. I also felt that healing had begun on my tooth again during the dream state, too.*

'This has never happened to me before. I do receive visions from time to time but have never had an experience like this before.'

I had a similar incident happen, and although in hindsight some aspects of it were very funny, it also taught me some valuable lessons when it comes to positive energy and how hard it is to have when you're in pain. It also taught me that being positive, no matter what the provocation, really is the only way to *be*.

Tony and I had decided to take our fairly newly acquired motor home up to the Lake District from our home in Somerset. We were going to do the journey in three stages, stopping off three times at three different campsites, and then arrive at Lake Windermere in time to meet Tony's brother and sister-in-law and spend a few days with them. On the last night before we set off I was awakened by a toothache, the worst I'd ever known. It was so bad that my whole mouth hurt and it was hard to decide which exact tooth was causing the problem. But I filled myself with positive intent and told myself it would go. I really didn't want to spoil or delay the holiday. I also took some painkillers and by the morning the pain had gone. The next day we set off, but I was feeling quite stressed and had allowed myself to dwell on 'what if?' about the pain returning. After a few hours on the road my self-fulfilling prophesy came true and the pain started to come back. Tony offered to turn back for home, but it would have ruined the holiday and let his family down, so I pulled myself up and said that I'd take more painkillers and if the pain didn't ease we could find a dentist later on in the journey.

On the second night away the pain eased off and so we continued on. The second campsite was one of those where you never really know what you are going to find, but one thing we certainly didn't expect was that right behind our pitch a JCB (a sort of digger) would be working all day, going back and forth, back and forth ferrying loads of soil. It was very annoying and not at all what we'd paid for. I must admit it put me in a really bad mood and I got quite grumpy. I was still grumpy the next day and, sure enough, halfway to Southport the toothache returned with a vengeance. It was one of those pains I hope you've never experienced and never will experience, when you can't move, talk or think; you can only exist. Naturally this made me feel more negative, and the more I did that the worse, naturally, the pain became.

Of course it would have to be a Bank Holiday Monday, so all the dentists were shut. Tony phoned an emergency number and we were told that a dentist in a nearby town would reopen his surgery for a fee of £175! Well, there was nothing I could do, I couldn't exist another night and day with the pain, so we agreed. The reception desk told me that the town was about 5 miles away, so we decided I should get a taxi. That way Tony could stay on site in the motor home with our dog, KC. It seemed easier to do it that way rather than us all driving round a strange town in search of the dentist's, and trying to park our large vehicle there. Plus, of course a local taxi driver would know the way, wouldn't he?

The driver arrived 10 minutes late. I got in and we shot off. Literally. My mood was dark as he drove very dangerously, fast and 2 feet behind the car in front for the first several miles. Then he turned round and asked me, 'Do you know the way?'

Of course I said no, in no uncertain terms, feeling ever more negative, and we spent the next couple of terrifying miles with him driving one-handed and trying to look at a road map he held in the other hand. After a while I roused myself out of my self-pitying stupor enough to ask, 'How far is this place?' I felt that even my pain-induced state couldn't account for the time we were taking to cover 5 miles.

'About 15 miles,' came the answer. Now I had three problems: the pain, whether I'd get there on time to meet the dentist, and how much it was going to cost for the taxi ride now that it was three times the expected distance. I only had £20 on me. More negative thoughts. Throughout the journey from home it had never occurred to me that perhaps I was being shown that I really could create my own reality, and that negative thoughts attract negative outcomes. Also, I didn't think about the possibility that my angels, who were undoubtedly willing to help and had done a couple of times, couldn't get anywhere near my negative aura.

We emerged onto a very busy dual-carriageway. The driver began to regale me with exactly the sort of tales of his last visit to a dentist that you really don't want to hear when you're on your way to one! Realizing his mistake, he changed tack and started to boast to me about how he had run out of diesel the night before in his cab, and had filled up with vegetable oil direct from a chippy. He was very proud of the fact that he'd saved a lot of money by doing that. I was so sunk in my pit of despair that I barely registered what he was saying. The words were no sooner out of his mouth, though, when the taxi gave a little cough, then another, then it started to slow down. Oh, my God …

We ground to a halt on the very busy and dangerous road amid a cacophony of hooting from other drivers. The taxi driver rested his head briefly in his hands and then got out of the car and walked around the back. I looked out of the window incredulously to see him trying to thumb a lift! He was going to dump me there! I jumped out of the car while phoning Tony on my mobile to tell him I was stranded at the roadside and thumbing a lift.

There was stunned silence as I asked him to try and call the dentist to tell him I *was* still on my way!

Just then a little saloon car pulled up next to the driver.

'I'll give you £10 to take me to a garage,' he announced to the family in the car. There were already four people in the tiny car, so I didn't know where he was going to sit, but he pushed his way inside somehow. I stepped forward, my shock at the driver's actions giving me a feisty feel, and said, 'I'll give you £10 to take me to the dentist!'

The family in the car were Good Samaritans and also obviously really in need of this unexpected £20 bonus, so they all moved over and, amazingly, I squeezed into the backseat with the wife, the teenage son and a baby. The husband and wife, bless them, didn't stop talking for the entire drive. The son, on the other hand, stared resolutely ahead, not speaking a single word. I came to think he was either a robot, or perhaps too freaked out by the chain of events to acknowledge what was going on. My thoughts amused me a bit and positivity saw a chink of light at the end of the tunnel. The car wheezed off, overloaded, the brakes doing that slidey thing they sometimes do every time we came to a corner, which seriously suggested the car couldn't have recently passed an MOT. My spirits lifted a little more as we progressed down the road, but I had no idea if we'd ever find the dentist. The thought of missing him now was too much to bear.

Of course no one in the car really knew where we were going, and it looked hopeless. I finally did what I should have done before: I centred myself, banished bad thoughts and pain, and asked for angelic help. Seconds later we were passing an elderly woman walking along, and I just knew she was my answer. I shouted above the conversation, 'Ask her!' It turned out we were just around the corner from the dentist's. Yippee! I handed over the £10 quite happily, and moments later I was deposited outside a building with a brass nameplate on it – but there was no one there. I watched my good Samaritans driving off. My heart sank again a little as I plunged again into a negative abyss. I'd thought I was getting some help at last. Had I missed him after all? Then a car pulled in, but I still felt wretched. A man, and a woman carrying a baby, emerged from the car. The man, who was indeed the dentist, said, 'I'm really sorry but I've just realized that the keys to the surgery are in my wife's car, and we've come in mine. I live 45 minutes away. I'll have to go back for the keys.' That was it. The end. I burst out laughing. I couldn't help myself. The situation had become so dire I had no choice but to laugh. They all looked at me incredulously, even the baby.

It was like a cloud lifted. The laughter caused a stream of positive energy and finally the day turned my way. The dentist realized that instead of driving home he could go to his business partner's home, which was just nearby, and borrow his keys, which he did. The pain suddenly became removed from me. It was still there, but detached, and even the last little joke in the farce didn't faze me –

when we got inside the electricity was off. But, finally I got my tooth fixed, and then of course I just had to find my way back to the campsite, and I certainly didn't fancy another taxi. But of course by now the angels were with me, and the dentist immediately offered to give me a lift to the train station. A lovely little train took me back to Southport, and a very short taxi ride saw me back at the campsite, where Tony and KC were anxiously waiting.

It was only later that, thinking about the entire thing, I realized that it had been a real roller-coaster of negative and positive mind-sets, with the appropriate bad and good things happening to coincide directly with them. It taught me a valuable lesson: no matter how impossible things seem, positive energy *can* and will make a difference. Tony, KC and I went on to the Lake District with no further incidents, and enjoyed the rest of the holiday.

ANGELS PREVENTING ACCIDENTS
This came from Lindy:

'I know I have my guardian angel around me all the time and he has been looking after me to the point where I can become quite carelessly complacent while driving. One day I was driving along a familiar route home and I had to make a left turn across an intersecting road. People who are not familiar with the suburb where I grew up don't realize that there are two roads intersecting right before a T-junction, and on many occasions I have seen near-misses

between vehicles. As I was driving, I was singing along to the radio, not paying any attention to the road and going quite fast to boot. Suddenly I heard a voice say "Stop!" and I immediately braked. I was just going around the blind corner and, as I did, there in front of me and about to cross my path was a car driven by a learner driver. She stopped also and for a moment we sat there looking at each other, then I waved her on because she had right of way. I got goose-bumps and thanked my angel, because if he hadn't told me to stop I would have T-boned this car.

'I have had many instances where I have been driving and heard a voice to tell me to slow down, change lanes, stop, etc., and if I hadn't listened I would have been in an accident. I even got told by a clairvoyant some years back that I should pay more attention while driving because my angel was getting sick of looking out for me and one day he would have had enough! That was an eye-opener for me!!!'

Lynn sent me her account of how angels stepped in and saved her from a car wreck:

'I was 16 at the time, and I was going out with a guy who was in the RAAF [Royal Australian Air Force]. His best mate was also a "raffy", and lived down the road from my house. My boyfriend came from an RAAF base in Sydney, and would travel up a lot to hang out with his best mate, who was stationed up here in the Newcastle area. In fact, that's how I met my boyfriend in the first place.

'Gary was my boyfriend's name (I later married him, but lost him in an accident three years after we were married and when I was eight months pregnant with our son). Dave was his best mate's name. Dave had a girlfriend by the name of Robyn, who came from a town up the coast. It was Easter time, and the Sydney Royal Easter Show was on, so Dave, Gary and I were going to go up to Robyn's town to go on a coach trip with her from there to the Sydney Show.

'My mum was a bit worried about it, but she finally agreed to me going. Finally, we were all set, so we left from my home and went to a petrol station in my suburb to fill up with fuel for the trip to Robyn's, which was about an hour and a half away.

'I was sitting in the back waiting for the boys to come back to the car and I was feeling a bit weird. I was known to have these feelings and as I sat there I was saying to myself, "It's all OK. We have money, we have food, we have fuel, it's all fine, we will be fine," then I went to put my seatbelt on to be ready when the boys got back in the car. But as I went to put it on, a voice, a male voice, inside my head, said, "Don't put it on," which was very weird because we have the use of seatbelts drummed into us. But when you hear something like that, someone talking to you inside your head, you can't help but obey!

'I felt uneasy then, and it felt so weird to have heard a voice in my head. Anyway, the boys came back, I kept my seatbelt off, which felt a bit wrong, and off we went. Everything was going along normally, but I was feeling anxious *and just wanted to get there and be safe, as the weird feeling I'd been having was getting stronger.*

'We were going through a place called Raymond Terrace, and just outside that, where the freeway restarted, was what was called the "mad miles". It was called that because once everyone got out of Raymond Terrace the highway opened up and everyone used to just "go go go"! As it was Easter, the traffic was incredibly heavy coming down towards Newcastle. We were going north, but the southbound traffic was bumper to bumper, very, very heavy but still moving at a decent pace. I smoked at the time, and as I was nervous I took a cigarette out and was about to light it when I just had this incredibly strong feeling not to. I didn't hear a voice this time, but I might as well have, because the force that was stopping me wasn't me. I put the cigarette away and was getting really scared, as there were a lot of trucks going in the opposite direction and every time one went past I'd cringe.*

'I was stressed. Then, all of a sudden, Gary yelled to Dave and pointed to the front of Dave's car. All he got out was, "Watch out for the …!"

'Then all I knew was that there was a huge crunch, a flip and a twist, and we ended up spinning down the road on the roof of the car, upside down. People who've almost died sometimes say, "I saw my life pass before my eyes." Well, I really did, and it was incredible! As I was tumbling around in the back of the car, seatbelt-less, I could see my life pass before my eyes, from when I was a baby all the way to where I was then. It was like looking at negatives from a camera; each pane has a different picture, with all those holes top and bottom so it can be held in the camera. It was just like that, and each pane had a different part of my life, all running very smoothly past my eyes. I know it sounds weird, but that was what I saw. Very interesting, really!

'The car finally came to a stop. Gary was able to get out of the car, and I could hear him, sounding very stressed, trying to get the people who'd gathered around to put their cigarettes out, because there was a whole tank-load of petrol streaming out everywhere. Dave and I were stuck in the car, and Dave was pretty badly injured. I was squeezed into this tiny squashed space in the back, and couldn't get out. Luckily I hadn't lit that cigarette. One shudders to think what would have happened if I had.

'It turned out that a young 16-year-old who'd only had his bike licence for two weeks had been riding a brand new 650CC Yamaha and decided to come down from much further up the coast, the opposite way to us. He'd been travelling with a friend who was way, way behind him, going at a much more sensible speed. The reckless Yamaha rider had been car-hopping all the way down, taking risks, his friend said. He'd then come out from behind a big semi-trailer (hence my fear of them on the way) and crashed right into the front of our car, on the driver's side, which in turn pushed us into the semi, then flipped us over and sent us spinning down the road. The roof of the car was so damaged and squashed that it had moved over to the right.

*My Gary burnt one of his fingers down because he was try-
ing to hold the roof up so hard that he actually had one of
his fingers pressed onto the road, not the roof. If I'd had my
seatbelt on I would have been dead. Instead of my being
tossed away, my head would have collided with the road,
and my head would have been worn down by the road as
we skidded along! But because I didn't have it on, I'd been
thrown into the middle of the backseat, where I'd been rela-
tively safe. (So long, that is, as the petrol hadn't been ignited
by the cigarette I'd wanted to light.)*

*'The 16-year-old of course was, sadly, dead, and his mate
was devastated. He told us then about the car-hopping and
taking risks and going crazy.*

*'We later took pictures of the car once it had been taken to
the wrecker's, and our friends would come and have a look
at it too. It had been just opened up by the bike and truck
like a tin can, and it was so squashed and broken, no one
could believe any of us had gotten out alive. There was no
room for us to survive in that car, but we did with the grace
of God and huge help from our darling angels and guides. I
like to think it was the Archangel Michael who spoke to me
that night. I would really love to know for sure.'*

Des sent me this story of an angel that definitely seems to
have used a bird to save Des' life.

*'Approximately eight years ago we had family visiting us in
Ireland from the United States.*

They stayed for three weeks in Derry, which is about 150 miles from Dublin. When the time came for them to head back to the US, as there were about 12 of them we needed three cars to ferry them back to Dublin Airport. As their flight was leaving Dublin that morning at 9 o'clock, we had to be on the road for about 3.30 a.m.

'We were about 20 miles from Dublin and everything seemed to be on schedule. I was driving the middle car of our three-car convoy. I was very tired and I must have suddenly closed my eyes and dropped off to sleep. Almost instantly I was woken up by the sound of a loud thud on the windscreen. My eyes flew open to see a bird caught in my screen wipers. I slammed on the brakes and just about managed to slow my car down, regain control and pull in at the side of the road.

'The third car in our group immediately pulled up behind me, and when the driver reached us he said that he'd really thought we were all goners, as my car had been travelling diagonally along the road at speed straight towards a clump of trees. Had it not been for that bird we would have been, at the very least, seriously injured, as I'd been driving at about 60 mph. I realized then that the four passengers in my car had been dozing, too.

'In all the years I've been driving and all the years since that incident I don't think I've had a bird fly across my windscreen, let alone hit it and become entangled in my wipers. Also, this happened about 5.00 a.m. when you wouldn't expect birds to be flying around anyway. This is

*a full and honest account of an incident that happened to
me, and I believe my guardian angel was there that night.'*

ANGELS PROTECTING THE VERY YOUNG OR WEAK

I've already said that angels help everyone, no matter what
their age, and I've often had bereaved parents come to me
for reassurance after the loss of a child or baby, which is
always of course terribly tragic and traumatic. So I was
very pleased to talk to Ann, who told me this wonderful
story.

*'I was lying in bed next to my husband, in the dark, just
a little light filtering through the curtains. I put my hands
flat on my belly, relishing the life I could sense inside me. I
was 24 weeks pregnant with my second baby, and so happy. I'd been trying for a baby for some time, and yearned
to have this feeling. Then, suddenly, everything changed.
Something made me aware of a presence beside my bed and
I opened my eyes, but that was all I could do. To my terror
I realized I was unable to move at all. I tried very hard to
move myself, but couldn't. I was really scared because beside
my bed stood a man. He was dressed really strangely, in a
buckled mackintosh and with a trilby hat pulled down over
his face. He reminded me of an old-fashioned movie private
detective, the way he was dressed. I felt my panic grow as
I tried to move and sit up but couldn't. I was paralysed
and my body wouldn't respond to anything I wanted it to*

do. I strained my eyes sideways to look at my husband, who remained asleep. The man just stood and looked down at me, and although I could not see his face I took it to be a kind one, as I felt very calm all of a sudden. This was odd because my intuition told me he was something to do with my baby. I lay there motionless as he reached his arms out to me. The next thing I knew was that it was morning, and almost immediately my waters broke prematurely and I lost the baby. The man in the trilby hat kept coming into my mind, and I couldn't stop thinking he was somehow connected to this.

'I was terribly upset, of course, at the loss of my baby, but I got pregnant again within a year and soon I was 24 weeks in again. One night the same man again appeared to me beside my bed. I couldn't move again, and I was filled with hopelessness as I knew he was coming to take my baby again. But, it was really weird, because although I was distraught at the thought of losing another baby, I still felt an underlying calm from this man, as if what was going to happen was meant to happen, and I shouldn't fight it. On awaking the next day, I prepared myself for the worst. Again I lost the baby, in the same way as before, but I was expecting it to happen this time.

'Needless to say I was devastated and extremely distressed about all that had happened, but felt that the man in the hat was looking after my babies. I felt that rather than stealing them he had been somehow coming to give me a warning and also comfort that he was waiting to take care

of them. I went through a bad year, but eventually I got pregnant again and this time was given a stitch in my cervix to hold the baby when it got to a certain weight.

'Naturally, as 24 weeks approached I got very scared. I was walking on eggshells and felt like a living time-bomb. One night I was asleep and I was woken by something I can only describe as an orange glow. At first I thought, "Oh no! Not again!" But then I realized that this time it was different. Instead of the man in the hat, there was just a gentle glow beside the bed. I tried to wake my husband but he would not stir. The light got bigger and a lovely warm feeling of peace and serenity emanated from its centre. As the light got bigger, in the centre I saw what I can only describe as a beautiful smiling face. It seemed to fill the room, and then I saw the outline of what I would call an angel, with large wings, dressed as I would imagine an angel should be.

'This angel seemed to hover in mid-air, and I heard the words, "Everything is well, you will be fine," and then it was gone. I felt very emotional and just knew that I would have my baby and all would be well, as the angel had said. Alex, my son, was born early at 32 weeks into my pregnancy, but I never had a moment's fear or doubt that he would survive, and indeed he did.

'The interesting footnote to this story is that when I was telling others about the experience in a workshop, two people said that they both had lost babies and had both seen this man in a hat beside their bed just before it happened. They both described him to me exactly! In hindsight we all

> felt he was an angel of some sort who came to take care of
> lost babies.'

I hope this story will help all those mums and dads who have lost their little ones to see that no soul is ever truly lost or abandoned. This wonderful story also confirms to me my theory that the same baby will often come back several times, to be lost again, just because they're always going to have a difficult time being born alive, and these 'rehearsals' are their way of strengthening their connection to their parents in both body and soul, so that at last they will survive the process and be born healthy. This story is an important one because it also demonstrates how angels can appear in a vast variety of forms.

ANGELS THAT HELP WHEN A LOVED ONE MUST LEAVE US

Guardian angels can come into our lives at any time, but quite often the first time is one of great change and upheaval, and sometimes sadness that evolves into a gift. So it was with Laura Lyn:

> 'During one summer night, my papa took me to a Memorial Day celebration near a large lake. He prepared me in advance for all the noise and ruckus from the fireworks. He told me that each "boom" and beautiful colour represented an angel, and the bigger the boom, the closer the angel. Together we counted the booms, and soon lost count.

The noise continued, and I was mesmerized by the bursts of light against the dark sky and the reflection of the bright lights against the lake.

'In my mind there was an angel for each splendid display in the sky, and another one for its reflection in the lake. After the grand finale, Papa hugged me and said, "There are over 10,000 angels by your side that will always be with you."

'The first time I saw my Guardian I was lying in bed next to my sister. I remember basking in the contentment of the previous several days, when I'd spent time with my grandparents. I was looking up at the ceiling and a purplish glow in the right-hand corner caught my eye. I felt instant comfort and peace, and quickly realized this was my angel. I soaked up as much of the energy as I could muster. I hummed, and heard a sharp-pitched vibration resonate back towards me. I felt we were in loving communication with each other.

'I looked nightly for this wonderful glow, and felt certain disappointment if I did not achieve the vision. One night the glow grew brighter and brighter and revealed itself to me, growing very large and luminous. The angel had on what appeared to be, in my childish eyes, a luminous wedding dress, surrounded with hues of purple, blue and lavender. I watched in amazement as the glow transformed into an angel and filled up the entire bedroom. I felt very comforted, as if I were wrapped cosily in a large overstuffed blanket. As the angel revealed herself I could not see her *face, but she had two beautiful crystal blue eyes, from which rays of light shone.*

'The angel had a sombre message, and informed me that my grandfather would soon be going away. I nodded and accepted the message. To me, "going away" meant going on a trip. The angel promised she would always be with me. Two weeks later my grandfather died, and from that day on, and my life changed for ever.

'My angels have helped me all my life, bringing messages to others. I am grateful towards my papa for bringing their light to me.'

This story came from Linda, and demonstrates how angels can often allow us glimpses into the spirit world at times when we really need to say goodbye to someone and yet can't be physically by their side:

'I'd come down from Norfolk to visit my parents in their home in Maidenhead. I was alone in the house with my baby son, Simon. It was a bright, normal day and I was busy changing his nappy when the front door-bell rang. My hands were full and I couldn't leave my son alone on the table in case he rolled off, so I called out to my visitor to ask if they could please wait a few moments. I then pinned the fresh nappy on my son, put him safely in his pram and went to see who was ringing the bell. I went to the front door and opened it, just in time to see the unmistakable figure of my father-in-law turn the corner at the end of the gravel

drive and disappear behind a tall hedge. I was about to call out his name and run after him, when I stopped cold. The complete improbability and impossibility of the situation struck me.

'*My father-in-law, Jack Hutchinson, was a genial, open-hearted ex-policeman, and was in many ways the complete opposite of his brooding son, my then-husband Daniel. Jack and I had grown very close during my marriage to his son (which ultimately failed), and I was very fond of him.*

'*The reason I'd stopped, shocked, at the front door that day, instead of calling out and running after Jack, was because I knew that he was in Norfolk suffering from terminal lung cancer, with Dan by his side. There was no way Jack could have been in Maidenhead, 200 miles away.*

'*Shortly afterwards Dan phoned to say that his father had passed away, and I knew that dear Jack had come to say goodbye to me.*'

This incredibly beautiful story comes from Tricia:

'*My mum lost my little brother, Toby, when he was only about 17 months old, some 35 years ago. He was a late baby, born when my mum was in her forties and I was already 20. She found Toby still and lifeless one morning. It was a cot death, but that didn't make it any easier. He'd been sickly since he'd been born very early, but that didn't help either. In the night I'd hear her crying, and Dad trying to soothe her. I thought her heart would break. I thought she'd die, too, from the grief. She felt very guilty and she'd cry out that he was alone now, and she needed to know if he was OK.*

'One day when she was really down she told me that in the night he'd died she'd been woken up – maybe he'd made a noise, she'd been too sleepy to know for sure. She said she'd thought she saw the lit-up figure of a man standing in the corner of the room. He held out a hand to her and smiled sadly. She thought he was carrying a bundle in his arms. She'd slipped back to sleep while she was seeing it, and thought later it was a dream. After the next day's events, though, she thought an angel had come to warn her that Toby was ill, and she'd ignored it. That was why she felt so guilty. What kind of a mother, she asked, would ignore an angel trying to warn her to check on her baby? I tried to console her, but it didn't work. She never told Dad, I guess because she thought he might blame her, too.

'Then something happened. It was right after the funeral, when we'd had to watch that little coffin being lowered into the ground. Mum suddenly cheered up. She was still sad and still cried a lot, but it was more just like tears spilled out of her eyes, rather than the hysterical heaving that had gone on before. Eventually I broached the subject, gently asking if she felt a bit easier. She turned to me with tears glistening in her eyes, and joy, actual joy, gleaming there. She told me that at the funeral she'd looked across the grave to see the same man she'd seen in the night, standing there in broad daylight. He'd smiled and pointed behind him

and over to a tree. There on the grass in the shade was Toby, crawling around and gurgling happily. My mum said she took a step, wanting to run to Toby, but the man shook his head, no, and mouthed at her, "He'll wait for you." With that the spell was broken and the man and my brother dis-appeared. Mum said after that she knew that Toby was safe and being looked after. She never told Dad about that ei-ther, because he was a bit cynical about that kind of thing. She didn't want him to spoil it for her and make her doubt, I think.

'My mum passed away unexpectedly five years ago. The night after she died my dad said he'd had the weirdest dream the previous night. He said he'd thought he was awake, but couldn't have been because he saw a young man standing in the bedroom door. He was all lit up and smiling. He said there was a man standing behind the boy – and he was lit up too. In the morning he forgot about it, and Mum col-lapsed suddenly later in the day. She never even made it to hospital.

'That evening was when Dad told me about his dream. I felt I had to try and explain, and I told my dad about what had happened years ago when Toby died. I told him that I thought the man was the angel who'd been caring for Toby, and that the young man was Toby. He'd said he'd come back for Mum.'

I've come across this kind of story before (there are some in *Angel Whispers*); it appears that there are special angels that come to collect babies ready to pass over. The man varies slightly, but he's similar enough for the stories to give credence to each other.

ANGELS THAT STEP IN TO HELP UNEXPECTEDLY

Mandy is a radio presenter. In a world of media where the spiritual is often left on the back-burner, or treated less than seriously, she's quite rightly proud of the fact that on her show she features spiritual teachers from around the world. This entails her making recordings with them at odd times, as they're often on the west coast of America, whereas her studio is in the UK. Much to her disappointment, one day she was informed by her bosses that she would no longer be able to do these telephone hook-ups. This was a big upset for her, and she felt quite down about it. Her boss wasn't always the easiest person to discuss this kind of thing with. Mandy then did one of my focus pictures (as instructed in *Angel Whispers*) and felt an immediate change in her energy. She decided to take this matter philosophically, and with gentle energy said to her boss that afternoon, 'So, I guess I won't be able to do my 4 p.m. phone hook-up today.' From previous information she was pretty sure that she already knew the answer and it would be in the negative, but to her surprise her boss said, 'Of course you can, why shouldn't you?' And he proceeded to set it up for her. The previous decision was apparently totally forgotten!

Coralline writes to tell me this story of her unexpected angel saviour:

'*My mom told me about the time when I was about 3 years old. She was taking me to the candy store a few blocks from our house, which was on a busy street in Tucson, Arizona. We were waiting at the roadside to cross, and Mom says she doesn't know what happened but suddenly I slipped my hand from hers and started running into the street. I guess I was in a real hurry to get some candy! She says she stood frozen as I passed in front of some cars, and drivers started to slam on their brakes. She saw me nearly reach the other side of the street, and then she saw the truck that was bearing down on me as I toddled on oblivious. By then she was screaming my name, but knew she'd never reach me in time and felt helpless, watching the tragedy unfold.*

'*The truck driver said later he couldn't even see me in the road, I was so small and he was so close. Just as the truck grille, on a level with my head, was about to hit me, Mom says a blinding white light flashed over my head. It threw me to the ground, and the truck bulk passed right over my body. Certain I was dead, Mom unfroze and ran screaming across the street. The truck driver saw in his rear-view mirror the woman running towards a small bundle, and he braked at last. He jumped out and ran back to us. By now traffic was pulled up all over the place. He found my mom hugging me, unable to speak. I was completely untouched. She couldn't believe it and neither could the driver. To this day she says an angel saved me.*'

There were several strange accounts that came back from the trenches of the First World War. I'm sure the angels must have had their hands full trying to prevent deaths that weren't meant to happen, for I'm certain that God in his wisdom never meant for so many millions to die in an act of man against man. Several young men, crouched in the mud of their trench, have told of how they were terrified to 'go over the top', and some of them never did. More than one told of how they suddenly saw a glorious figure of light rise into the air above the fallen dead, and that it beckoned to them. Unable to resist, they scrambled from the apparent relative safety of their trench and ran towards the heavenly figure. Seconds later the trench they'd been sheltering in suffered a direct hit, and there was no doubt that, had they remained in it, they would have been killed instantly. Those men came back alive.

Still I hear some people saying, 'I ask and ask for my angel to help me, but nothing happens.' They also wonder why others seem to get help without really trying, and yet they try and don't. Well, of course, some, like the young soldiers above, get help because they aren't meant to die, and some people get help because they're more open and connected than they might appear on the surface. I ask people who doubt to look deeply into their lives, and almost always they recall some incident, maybe minor, when they *did* get a helping hand unexpectedly, but dismissed it as just a bit of luck.

It's a small start, but once you do begin to believe, anything is possible. The problem is that often we let our logical left brains take over and get in the way, dismissing what we see as meaningless coincidence. So, next time something a little 'odd' happens, make a note of it and suspend your disbelief. It really is true that the more we allow the little things to open our minds and instil a childlike sense of wonder in us, the more angels can get through and the more signs, and bigger, they can send.

ANGELS ARE OUT FOR YOUR OWN GOOD

'Does my angel hate me?' some ask. No, of course not, and angels would find the concept of hate impossible to comprehend anyway. What happens is that people become caught in a downward spiral of despair when it seems their lives are going wrong and falling apart all around them, until they get so caught in a maelstrom of negative energy that they simply repel their angels like an opposite magnetic field would. It becomes impossible for an angel to get near them, let alone help them. In these cases the person has probably started this sorry state of affairs by taking a wrong path on their life's journey. A door has been slammed quite forcefully in their face by their guardian angel in an attempt to herd them back onto their rightful path. This has been misinterpreted as 'bad luck', the person fights against it (and therefore their angel and their destiny) and the resulting run of what seems to be incredibly bad luck continues. When this happens the only course of action is to stop, think, understand that you're going the wrong way and pushing for the wrong things, accept that your angel is trying to stop you for your own good, and look around for an alternative opening, because there *will* be one. Your angel will never lead you into a dead end, so if you find yourself facing one, then you've taken yourself there by not listening and refusing to be led down another route. The way out can be as simple as meditating and asking your angel to show you the right way. The signs will come.

CHAPTER 3

MASTER PATH ANGELS

Angels guide us to become spiritual people for the pleasure of it ... because the spiritual life itself has a great deal of beauty and real satisfaction, even pleasure. And this is what the soul needs. – **Thomas Moore**

Master path angels are those who can make truly amazing life changes happen for us. Some people call them Archangels, but I prefer my term as it seems to fit them better.

We all come to this life with a goal, or maybe many, and we all have a purpose and a role to fulfil, and finding it will make us truly happy. The happiness that comes from fulfilling our purpose is true happiness. Unlike the transient happiness we get from material possessions, the joy we get from being in the right place, the place we were destined to be, doing the right thing, the thing we were destined to do, cannot be removed from us no matter what befalls us. Master path angels are the ones who can help us find our niche and therefore our inner happiness.

The key to getting help from these angels is to take the path of least resistance. As humans we often want what we want, and not what we *need*. Or we tend to ask angels for help and then make the mistake of trying to force them into helping us to our ends in the only way or at the only time that we can imagine. This is the biggest cause of problems when it comes to our master path angels.

This is just one of my personal experiences that demonstrate how this works. My husband Tony and I wanted to move back out of the town, where we'd moved for work, to the countryside where we'd always felt at home. We saw a bungalow advertised in a nice village and thought it might fit the bill. It looked really lovely. We made an appointment to meet the estate agent there. We pulled up outside a little early, so we got out of the car to look around. From the outside the house looked perfect and very pretty, with painted shutters that added a certain charm to what was otherwise a modern home (we wanted modern this time, having had a period money-pit in the past!) and we could tell that it would have a very nice view from the back garden. However, I was drawn to walk further down the hill. I had no idea why, but I followed this path of 'least resistance'. I did what I tell other people to do: I 'made like a sheep' and 'followed' my intuition, which is another way of saying I heard and attended to what my angel was telling me.

Further down the hill was another bungalow with another estate agent's sign outside. It was less pretty, having been painted a dull battleship grey with a mustard garage door. It had no shutters, and so was a lot plainer. I thought, in my logical left brain, *this is not so nice*. But in my intuitive right brain I was told, *just look closer.* One of the things we really wanted in our new home was a big garden, especially as we have a very lively dog. We wanted a bit of space around us, unlike the cramped town layouts. We felt that spiritually we'd be better that way. So, when I looked over the wall into the back garden of the second bungalow (from the church car park next door), and saw a whole acre of garden stretching down to the stream at the bottom, I fell in love with it. However, it seemed pretty obvious to us that this bungalow was going to be out of our price range. Still I heard that voice, *just look.* So, using my mobile, I called the agents on the board and asked if we could view the second house in about half an hour. Amazingly they said yes, they could have someone out there that quickly.

We went back to the first bungalow then, as the agent for that one had arrived, but I confess it had lost a lot of its charm for me by then. We looked around, politely, but all the while we were thinking about the other one. When we were finally shown around the garden of the second bungalow, Tony and I still had no idea of the price, and we silently mouthed to each other, *there's no way we can afford this.* When the agent finally handed us a set of the details, we could see that in fact it was about 20K out of our price range, even if we were to get a good price for our old home in the town. To say we fell in love with the house and its idyllic location would be an understatement. I loved the conservatory where you could sit and look down the garden. I loved the raised patios that made the terraces of the garden accessible. I loved the spacious rooms and the quirky kitchen. I loved it all. Of course there was the little matter of it being out of our price range, and us definitely not wanting a mortgage, but we put that out of our heads, confident that our house would sell quickly for a top price and we'd be able to afford to buy our dream home. Six weeks later we hadn't had even one offer. I'd heard my angel, I'd listened and reacted, and yet our house hadn't sold at all, and the devastating phone call we'd dreaded had come, telling us the bungalow we'd set our hearts on was sold.

Time went by and we had very little interest in our house, and very little interest in looking around at other houses for sale. What was my angel playing at? This is what I mean when I say we tend to have limited imaginations about how and when, and the best ways for angels to help us. We couldn't understand why we hadn't got a buyer in time. Surely it would even have been worth accepting a lower offer and borrowing the balance, putting ourselves in debt, if it had meant we could get that bungalow. It was where we were meant to be, we were certain.

We tried looking for another house that was as nice, but of course we couldn't find one. We thought about buying the first bungalow we'd been to see that day, but we couldn't imagine living just a few doors up from where we really wanted to be. Many people reading this will have been sent on wild goose-chases by agents, to find that the property they were sent to was nothing like what they wanted. So it was with us. After a particularly annoying visit to a bungalow with a factory practically in the back garden, after we'd asked for serenity, we found ourselves driving back to town right past our wished-for home. As we passed by, both unable to resist a longing glance at it, I was suddenly hit with a few words from my angel, and I repeated them to Tony: 'Don't worry, it's coming back on the market.'

We finished the journey in high spirits, certain all was going to work out, putting aside, with trust, the fact that our house still hadn't had any offers made on it, and that the bungalow was still too expensive for us.

The next day I got an email from the agent to say that the house was indeed back on the market. The very next day, after months of trying, we got a buyer. When I told the agent what had happened, he asked me what time I had told Tony about the message. I answered that it had been about 3 p.m. The agent was flabbergasted because that was the very time that he had received the call telling him the previous buyer had had to withdraw! Not only that, but although we didn't get quite what we wanted for our house, the bungalow's seller was now in a position where he had to move right away, and so was willing to accept an offer below his asking price. So, no big borrowing and no getting into huge debt. Our angels had of course known best all along. One of the things Tony and I discussed after we'd moved in was how extraordinary it was that our new home hadn't had a string of buyers after it, which would have totally scuppered our chances of getting it for a reduced price.

Since moving here, so much good has happened. So be a follower, not a leader, when it comes to angelic help this powerful. You can never imagine the ways an angel might work and the path you might have to take to get where you want to be in life. So, if doors close in your face, look for an open window. Your master path angel will always give you a choice. If you decide instead to carry on banging your head against brick walls, you'll be allowed to do so – but the key is to look for the path of least resistance. If it seems easy, then it's meant to be.

ASKING FOR HELP

The way to ask these angels for help is quite simple. Be clear, keep it simple, ask for exactly what you want, but don't make any assumptions about how this end result is to be accomplished. Say thank you, and *let it go*. That last part is the hardest, I know. We have a tendency to nag our wishes, in the same way that we let our worries nag us. Nurture the dream, hold it close, keep it warm, visualize it, but don't pick at it. Trust the universe. This is necessary because, for one thing, we might always know what we want, but not always what we *need*. The universe and our angels will give us the best result for the best outcome. Leave it to them.

Here's an example of how master path angels can manoeuvre situations to put us in the right place at the right time, even though we don't realize that's where we are. It was reported in the United States and newspapers around the world that a woman from Arizona, Rita Van Loenen, had her life saved in a very bizarre moment of synchronicity. This woman was dying for the need of a working kidney. She had to take regular trips to the hospital to have dialysis, just to keep her alive. One day she told her taxi driver, Thomas Chappell, where she was going and why. Mr Chappell said he was a man of faith, and that right at that moment he felt a higher power urging him to make an incredible offer. He offered Rita Van Loenen one of his kidneys. He says that right then he knew that his kidney would be compatible with her, because the higher power told him so. Amazingly, he was right. Not only did he make the generous offer but he was found to have the right blood group and a compatible kidney. Rita Van Loenen said, 'There are better odds of getting struck by lightning. A random taxi driver offering to give me his kidney and all these pieces match. There has to be something behind this. How can this be?'

Laurence was living on the streets when he had this master path experience:

'This is the true story of what happened to me one morning when I thought I was going to die on the streets. It turned my life around. The road to homelessness is surprisingly short. One week you skip your rent to pay drug debts, or you get too drunk and blow all your pay, and before you

realize, the eviction notices start arriving at the door. When you end up homeless, it seems like there is no way out, but sometimes you get the chance to hear a different message.

'The lights of the city sparkled off the dark harbour looming below. I wondered what it would feel like to jump off into its dark waters beneath me. Would anyone miss me? How long, if at all, would it take until my corpse washed up on some wharf or jetty? Or would I just be consumed by a giant shark never to be seen again? These thoughts crossed my mind. The power of the city ground its successes into to my face as the corporate logos illuminated the night sky; I was reminded of who I was and what I had become. A gentle zephyr caressed my face, as if to comfort me. I plodded along regardless. I made my way down towards George Street until I got to Central railway station. It must have been around 4 a.m. The city was silent. I made my way into the tunnel that links Broadway to Liverpool Street. There was not a soul to be seen. Only the giant rats that lived in the underground walkway were awake, and they scurried away from me into the drains that line either side of the tunnel. My footsteps echoed through the silence interrupted only by the sound of the rats.*

'"Laurence!" a female voice called out of the silence. The only way to describe her tone of voice is "caring". Like when somebody who really loves you is trying to wake you up from a deep, deep sleep, so as not to frighten you.*

'I stopped and turned around to see who was behind me. There was nobody there, not even the rats! They'd all scur-*

ried off in fear of unexpected human intrusion. I checked myself. I must have been imagining things. I continued to walk as if nothing had happened.

"Laurence!" This time the voice was closer, louder and a little more serious, but still loving; as if to say, "Wake up!" That's it.

'I turned around again – still nobody in sight. "Who is it? Stop playing games! If you want something ... just ask!" My voice reverberated through the tunnel. No other sound or sight of another person could be seen or heard. I started to walk cautiously, expecting someone to jump me. I listened very attentively to my own footsteps and waited for the sound of somebody else's, as I continuously looked over my shoulder, hoping to surprise my attacker. "Laurence." This time the voice was right next to me. There was no one there, just the warm and comforting voice of what sounded like a beautiful woman; an angel.

'This was the turning point. After being homeless for six years, I started the long haul back into society, and now I'm making the world my oyster.'

It's interesting that the angel called Laurence by name, because angels don't see us as 'names', like we do, they only read our energy and recognize us from that. This is one of the reasons why I say that animals can sometimes be more spiritual than humans. Animals don't give each other names, they just recognize each other by their energy. But in communicating directly with us, as this angel did with Laurence, they understand that our names are crucial to us in identifying ourselves. We recognize ourselves in our names rather than in our own energy, so the angels know that they sometimes need to use the names we've given ourselves so we'll respond to the communication when it happens.

Here's Winifred's story:

'I'm certain I saw an angel once. I was going through a difficult time and was praying and crying. All at once I felt a power physically close my eyes. It was terrifying. I knew it was God wanting to show me something. I felt so insignificant, so small compared to this world and all the other worlds. What I grasped was this is a very, very short time (this life) and I felt we were like children playing in the sandbox at recess. This is a time for us to enjoy life.

'Well, to sum up, I was in a room, not just shown a room, I was there. It was full of women and children. I was afraid to look around because I thought they would know I was a stranger. The fear was very real. However, the women/children didn't notice me. I noticed their clothes were very colourful, without seams, and they were happy. It was a place of transition.

'Then a man appeared in the room. He was tall with grey hair and striking blue eyes. He was walking towards me and, as he approached, he read the question in my mind and answered, "Yes, I'm an angel. Do you want to touch me?" I was very afraid and somehow communicated "No."

'When I was crying and praying earlier I had been asking for an answer to a difficult question. The angel asked me, "What was your question?" The feeling I got instantly was about how insignificant my problems really were. I had an impression that the angel was an extremely busy being. He was in many, many different places and times. I felt so honoured and insignificant. When he leaned towards me, because he was very tall, his bright blue eyes shielded and sort of glazed over. I knew those eyes were more powerful than I could take. I asked my question (it was personal). He gave me an answer and the most outstanding advice I could've ever imagined. I wish I could have been strong enough to take it. This problem remains my nemesis. I'm weak spiritually.

'After he'd answered my question, I had so many others, but was afraid to ask because I felt too small in a sense, because he was so powerful. I knew he was leaving. He asked me if there was anything else. I said, "Yes, can I touch you?" I grabbed his arm and it was so warm and real. I instantly opened my eyes, and I was back at home with my arm outstretched. I knew I was given the biggest gift ever. I was on cloud nine for months, but being a weak person I shrunk back into superficiality.

'The clincher to this is that the angel was in blue jeans, cowboy boots and a belt with a big buckle. I wasn't on acid or under the influence of anything. I wasn't asleep. Anytime I've told someone, I've encountered sceptics. This was 14 years ago but very real. I know it happened. I would love for it to happen again.'

I can empathize with Winifred, because there's no doubt, once you've experienced being close to an angel, you always want more. How could you not? When I had my first experience of actually seeing, hearing and feeling an angel, in that moment I felt so alive, so unafraid, so content, so rapturous and so filled with the purest love that it has never left me. I hope that this angel returns at some point because, although it has sustained me through many years, and has been my unfailing talisman whenever any doubts have occurred, I'd still like to experience those things again in real time.

George told me this amazing story of how his life was changed in an instant:

'I was a street kid, a gang member. I won't say where or when, because gangs have long memories and even longer arms. We used to beat on people for kicks. I never really saw them as people. It was survival of the fittest as far as I was concerned. You beat on them before they beat on you. I'm not proud of what I did, but I was then. I wanted to be accepted, respected by the gang, because they were my brothers, and if they didn't accept me then who would? The law couldn't catch us – the only law we worried about was gang law. You didn't step on another gang's toes if you wanted to keep yours. I don't know where I would have ended up if things hadn't changed. Maybe I'd be dead, in prison, or maimed like I maimed others. We always went around in packs, always acted in packs.

'I'll never know for sure what made that night different. I was out on my own. I wasn't scared because I was well inside my gang's territory, so nobody, I mean nobody, was going to mess with me. Not even the law. The cops would steer round me.

'There was only one thing stranger than me going out alone, and that was whatever the reason that "she" was out alone, too. I couldn't believe it when I saw her. She must have been 80 years old, dragging a shopping cart behind her. It was in a really bad part of town. She wasn't a bag lady – too well-dressed. Her hair done, make-up on despite her age. She was walking, bold as all get up, down one of the darkest alleys on the block. What was she doing there? I had no clue, but I knew one thing: She was rich pickings. The way she was dressed, she had to have a stash of cash in her bag. I could just swoop in there and grab it. If she resisted, well I had my baseball bat, didn't I?

'I walked right up to her, got in her face, grabbed her bag by the strap and yelled, "Give it up, lady! Just let go and I won't ... " To my amazement, not only did she not let go, but she started slamming my head with her umbrella. "Stupid cow!" I thought, and brought the bat up over my head. I swear to God I hit her really hard, but as the bat connected with her head it was like I'd hit steel. The bat vibrated so bad I had to drop it. I looked at her. There was this halo around her, sort of gold and white. Like she had a force field or something. It crossed my mind she was an alien. I jumped back to avoid the umbrella, which had *no trouble getting through the force field to hit me. She couldn't be an alien. If she was she'd look weird, or be wearing a space suit or something; she wouldn't be some old lady with a shopping cart! I didn't know what was going on, but I decided to run. It wasn't worth the hassle. I ran down the alley and, when I'd reached a safe distance, I looked back. There was no old lady, just a young woman in a gold cloak. She pointed at me and said my name, just that, "George …" quietly. Then the light and the woman just winked out. Gone.*

'*What could I do? I couldn't tell the gang. They'd think I was crazy, but I knew what I'd seen. I couldn't tell anyone. The next day I moved to another town. I was scared, yes, scared of the gang, because I sure as hell couldn't carry on the way we'd been, and I was scared of what I'd seen. My mom had moved away a couple of years previously, I guess to get away from me, so I tracked her down. She agreed to give me a second chance. I don't know what I saw that day – a space traveller, an angel or what – but now I feel like I have a future. Today I help out at a centre for people like I was, young guys stuck in a life they don't know how to get out of, and I talk to people who tell me the woman was an angel, sent to save me. They say I must be going to do something important with my life, that I'd gone down a wrong path and she came to steer me back. I don't know. We'll see.*'

I have no doubt that 'George's' experience was angelic. It will be interesting if I can keep tabs on him and see how he turns out, and what was so important about him that a master path angel stepped in, unasked, to save him from himself. Maybe he'll end up as the first ex-gang member to become President of the United States. Or maybe he'll be a father to someone who will change the world. Or maybe he'll just turn out to be a wonderful son.

CHAPTER 4
SOUL ANGELS

*If we ever wish to know angels for what they truly are ...
perhaps it is we who must first learn to fly.* – **Anonymous**

Do past lives impact on your current one? What are soul angels and how can they make you remember who you were before?

Many people are confused as to exactly what is meant by past lives and karma. A belief in past lives means an acceptance that we've lived before this life in another body, and that we will most likely live again by coming back in another body after our current one has died. The purpose of this is for our soul, that part of us which never dies, to learn and grow and evolve, by experiencing as many scenarios and group dynamics as possible that will teach us and expand our consciousness over many lifetimes.

The concept of karma is also misunderstood. The classic comment that demonstrates this is, 'I must have done something really bad in a past life to be living this one now!' People generally mistake karma for a judgement system, whereby we come back to life merely to atone for some misdeed in a past life. This isn't the case at all. Karma is about balance and knowledge. If there is an imbalance in our soul, whether it is caused by events or where there's a lack of knowledge, then we will come back primed to redress the balance and correct the omissions. Both of these things might involve living a less than perfect or even unpleasant life, but they are not meted out as punishment. Also, quite often if the lesson is understood and accepted during the current life, then the need for it has gone and life will improve. If the knowledge is learned and accepted, then the lesson is no longer needed and the pressure will ease.

People ask what happens after we've lived all the lives we need to on this plane. I didn't used to have an answer, but now I do. Eventually your soul will have learned enough and be balanced enough for it to move on to the next stage, a permanent reabsorbing into your root, which is angelic, as I'll explain in a moment.

A SPARK FROM AN ANGEL

My past-life story has been well documented, and the concept of soul angels expanded in my book, *Soul Angels*. These are the angelic beings that can be held up to demonstrate most easily that every single one of us does have angels to call on. There can be no doubt, because soul angels are the ones we are closest to when trying to come awake spiritually, and even more so because your soul *is actually a spark from a soul angel*. In fact *we* are soul angels, and *they* are us. Your soul was created from a fragment of the energy of a soul angel, and so your soul angel is there with you from the moment your soul was just a mere blank spark in the ground, right up to the current day.

A soul angel has accompanied you through all your lifetimes, and in between them, too. Your soul angel is the friend you discussed your previous life with each time it had ended, and who guided and helped you to choose the next appropriate lifetime for you to experience. The angel will have advised on location, era, parents, experiences, soul mate and soul clan connections, and also have allowed you to make contracts to help others of your group or be helped by them in order that you will encounter the experiences you need for your soul to progress. Why do they do this? Because these angels are the fount head from which our soul was born. They are the foundation from which our soul was chipped. Your soul is a part of them and they are your greatest part, so their evolution depends on yours.

ANGELIC 'NUDGES'

You are born into each lifetime without your memories intact, to face the challenge we all face in every life – to remain spiritual in the face of being human and all that brings, to reunite mind, body and spirit, and to reawaken to who you really are. The soul angel's role is to help you with this in any way it can.

Sometimes this help can seem a little cruel, as they will use any means possible to wake you up. They will be cruel if necessary, first so that you will 'wake up' and also so that you'll experience what you contracted to, even if in your human state you don't recall promising to do those things.

Sometimes these 'nudges', as I call them, will take the form or repetitive dreams or even nightmares. They can manifest as phobias, or even illnesses, or destructive behaviour patterns. Apparent 'bad luck' can nearly always be attributed to these angels. Why do they find it necessary to act so dramatically? Because, as I said, we are part of them and their evolution depends on being successful at waking us up, and our soul's evolution depends on their being successful at guiding us.

So, if you find yourself suffering from what seems like a particularly difficult life, take heart from the accounts in this chapter and see if you recognize yourself in any of these scenarios. If you do, then you've taken the first step towards changing things for yourself.

Remembering a past life by following the clues given by your soul angel is one of the quickest ways to wake up your soul. Doing so is the first step in the right direction towards the life you're meant to live.

If anyone had told me 15 years ago that I could be changed in a matter of months from a depressed, overweight, talentless, self-doubting mess into an award-winning, slim and confident song-writer and TV presenter, I would have laughed. If they'd told me that a few years later I'd be earning a living writing columns and books, I would have thought they were joking. But that's what happened. Back then, one afternoon, I had a soul angel reach me and, as I was in the right frame of soul, it was able to 'switch me on', and since then everything has changed.

One of the gifts I've been given is to be able sometimes to connect with a person's soul angel for them, and discover what their 'nudges' are all about. In this way I try to help them make first contact with their soul angel. Here are some of the answers I've been given.

Jean had a severe problem, which was having an impact on her relationship:

> *I'm terrified of having anything touching or covering my face. As my partner, James, likes to play with my hair as he goes to sleep, this causes me a lot of problems! Sometimes I have to get up and go downstairs and have a glass of water. I don't know if this is a past-life thing.*

Soul angel's answer:

> *'In a previous life you were sold into slavery by your poor French family. The slavers threw a sack over your head and carried you off. This was many lives ago, in the 700s, but you were so traumatized by the sudden and shocking transition from freedom to slavery, and the betrayal of your family, that your subconscious still feels that panic. So anything that feels remotely like a sack, anywhere near your head, is bound to make you desperate to escape. Now that you know this is in the past, you know this isn't going to happen to you*

again. Accept why you've been scared, and start to enjoy the loving touch of your partner.'

Maria had a health issue. These are often 'carry-overs' used by a soul angel to remind a person of some past life. In this case she needed to take the next step, which was to be regressed to that life by a qualified and experienced past-life therapist in order to heal the very real physical symptoms she was having:

I developed a 'weight-bearing' headache in 1997, and it just grew. Problems with my feet restrict me from walking properly. Diet and weight could be contributing factors, but I'm hoping you can help find a solution.

Soul angel's answer:

'In 1874 you were a housemaid in Cincinnati. At the age of 30 you were diagnosed with a terminal, infected ulcer, and because you were no more use to your masters, you found yourself in the clutches of a surgeon who used you to perform experimental brain surgery. One of these operations consisted of a hole being drilled into the top of your skull, so it's no wonder you are getting these headaches.

'You need to pay heed to this symptom and be regressed back to your life as this poor girl, and have the trauma healed. Once you have done that, your headaches, like your history, will fade into the past where they belong.'

Grace had a very nasty symptom, which leads me to expect that her soul angel had been giving her gentler nudges for some time, and that she'd been ignoring them. When this happens the soul angel has no choice but to raise the bar. Grace needed to recognize that her problems had past-life roots and live more open-eyed to past-life possibilities:

> *I wake up clutching my throat, convinced I've swallowed something. Once I thought I'd swallowed a mascara tube and I even tried to cough it up, until I realized it couldn't possibly be real. I never remember the rest of the dream that leads to the choking moment.*

Soul angel's answer:

> *'This was brought forward from a life in 1854, when you were a well-to-do American man named Solly. You choked on a piece of meat during a meal at home. It wasn't the form of the death, but the suddenness that caused your trauma. None of us knows when and how we are to die, but as you sat down to dinner on that evening you would never have suspected it was to be your last.*
>
> *'You need to bring your memories back while awake, through meditation, so that your subconscious doesn't need to remind you of it while you're asleep anymore.'*

Janice had a problem that was easily remedied by telling her where and when it came from. Usually when people are able to rationalize a fear, it immediately goes away:

I'm terrified of torch light. Their limited amount of light makes me feel like there's something lurking around me. I get very shaky and sometimes I close my eyes. I'd rather be in full darkness than with this small bit of light. I can't figure it out. I'm also really uncomfortable around children.

Soul angel's answer:

'You're going back a long, long way. This fear has been with you for too many lives to count, so it's about time you were able to heal it.

'Back in the times of cave-dwellers, you were a woman left at home to tend the fires and mind the children, while your "man" hunted. Minding the children was a big responsibility, and as darkness fell and he didn't return, you knew their father was dead. Animals prowled just out of reach of the firelight. The shadows played tricks, but you knew they were going to kill you and the children. Eventually you were picked off one at a time. No wonder you feel uncomfortable if left in charge of children now, and wavering lights make you feel afraid. We have no sabre-tooth tigers now, or wolves, or anything that's going to sneak up and get you, so you can relax at last.'

Sally needed to find what was missing in her life:

I've felt very empty inside since my childhood. What is it that is missing? I feel I want to go back to my past life, but don't know why. I feel I was very happy then. I'm drawn to Cornwall though I've never been there. Please can you see anything for me?

Soul angel's answer:

'Cornwall is definitely the priority area for you. I can see you dressed in a long blue skirt and a white puffy-sleeved blouse, standing on a green hillside or cliff-top above a place called Lamorna Cove. Day after day you stood, staring out to the sea at Mount's Bay, watching for your smuggler husband to return, but he never did. This life took place in the early 1800s, and if you ever get to Cornwall, either online or in person, and retrace your steps, you'll be able to heal the emptiness inside.'

Tracey wanted to know if her desire to act was related to a past life:

I'm just wondering if you see me ever becoming an actor? It's my heart's secret desire. Also I'm very interested in the Tudor era, and wonder if in a past life I might have been part of the court? I have vivid dreams about things in that time that I can't really know.

Soul angel's answer:

'In 1548 you died, aged 35. This wasn't young for that era. In fact you were pretty old for the time! Your name was

Catherine, and you were the governess to Elizabeth Tudor when she was a child. She called you by the pet name Kat.

'You should draw on all these memories and audition for any acting parts of people from that time, for you will surely beat all comers!'

Carrie's past life was hindering her from moving forward:

Could you tell me a little about my past life and what the future holds for me? I'm going through a rough patch at the moment and I'd like to know if things are going to get any better, and whether any of this is past-life related?

Soul angel's answer:

'In 1932 you were the first female teacher appointed to a European college. In this life your subconscious is blocking further education, feeling that a lot of your past life was wasted because, back then, women teachers weren't given the same respect as men.

'Now you know why you do it, you'll stop blocking and move ahead with what you want to do.'

Susie was having relationship issues:

All my life I've had bad dreams. I've also had bad luck career wise and am uncertain about the future. Can you see what my past life held? I'm particularly interested in the area of love and my current relationship (with Paul).

Soul angel's answer:

> *'In the early 1900s you were in love with a neighbour, Peter, who is now Paul. You tragically fell from a high window and were bed-bound from that day, which has caused you bad dreams in this life of being unable to escape from danger. Thinking Peter couldn't love you because of your condition, you refused to see him again. In this life he will try and reassure you that he does, and always did, love you, but you'll be hard to convince!'*

FAMILY ISSUES AND PAST LIVES

Family disagreements can be very complicated, because while they might appear to stem from flash-points in your current life, family members often reincarnate together, and so apparently simple arguments can often involve age-old resentments and feuds.

Soul angels can be called upon to resolve these issues, otherwise family members can go round and round in circles, always making the same mistakes and having the same issues. Your soul angel can help you sort out the confusion, either through meditation on your family members and their past lives, or by visiting a past-life therapist. I have a very comprehensive list of those available throughout the world on my website: www.jennysmedley.com.

George never did get on with his sister. From the moment she was born, when he was 2 years old, he seemed to resent her. Their mother felt she'd done everything she could to make sure he never felt superseded or replaced by the little girl, but it didn't help. George seemed to take pleasure in his sister's pain. If she were hurt or crying he'd grin and make his mother very angry.

When his sister got old enough to argue, it went from bad to worse and their mum was at her wit's end, constantly having to referee their fights and try to make them get along. The rows were always started by George, and this was making his mother actually start to dislike him. They were now both young adults and still not able to coexist, so their mum asked me to do a reading on them in one of my columns.

I called upon their soul angels to help and discovered an interesting story. This had been going on for many lifetimes. In one, George had been left to drown on a sinking ship, his sister being saved through the 'women and children first' tradition. In another life he'd been an old man, abandoned to die by his daughter (now his sister) when a fire raged through their house. In yet another life, George had been a fellow soldier (of his now sister) and had woken alone and dying on the battlefield, apparently left to die.

What George didn't know was that in the first life his sister had been dragged kicking and screaming from her brother to the lifeboat, and had been forced to leave him. In the second life she had only abandoned her attempts to save him because her child would have died without her help. It was a heartbreaking choice for her to make. In the third life (when she'd been a fellow soldier) she'd been knocked unconscious by a grenade and carried from the field that way, unable to make a choice.

Once George was reminded of all this, his memories of these events started to come back to him, and his subconscious' skewed version of those distant events was able to be rewritten. This greatly alleviated his animosity to his sister, and bridges were able to be built.

PAST-LIFE REGRESSION

While these messages I channel through from others' soul angels can be inspiring and in many cases have turned people around, I always tell them that at some point they should have past-life regression, which means recalling their past lives while under hypnosis, with the assistance of a good therapist. This is because while in some cases just having someone tell you about your past can help, there is no substitute for re-experiencing it for yourself. Also, you can have a therapist ask you prearranged questions so that you can get the specific answers you want.

What Happens Under Hypnosis?

You will be talked into relaxation. You'll still be aware of things around you, of the hypnotist's voice or any background noise, of light, but you won't interact with them. They'll be distanced. This feeling of relaxation may be all that happens on the first occasion, and you'll just feel pleasantly rested when it's over. If that's the case, don't worry, and don't think you're keeping something from yourself or that you're a failure. Instead, accept it as a first step. Once you get past this stage on the first or subsequent visit, you'll start to think of another time or place in your mind. When asked questions by the therapist, try to answer even if at that point what you're seeing and feeling don't seem real, or like just imagination. The block is usually released as soon as you start talking. Other knowledge and answers will just come to you. If this is all that happens, accept it as a step. Even if you feel you've just imagined things, it doesn't matter, because the magic of your reconnection to your soul has started.

The next stage will be a gradual slipping further into your past-life recall. In the end, if you go that far, you will feel totally immersed in it and won't doubt the reality. You'll actually be able to 'touch', 'taste' and 'smell' the past, and you'll certainly re-experience the emotions. Even through all this you won't be entirely unconscious, nor will you be under the control of the hypnotist or be unaware of what you're saying.

An experienced therapist will take you right through to your death in that past life, allowing you to look back at it from spirit, so taking away the fear that death is an end. Past-life trauma will be healed and you'll come back with new energy for this life, an understanding of who you really are and how you came to be that person, a deep connection to your soul and your soul angel, and an appetite and determination for the future.

DOUBT AND DISBELIEF

Sometimes people just refuse or don't seem able to listen to their soul angels no matter how hard they try. The 'coincidences' mount up and yet still their upbringing or their religious dogma, or plain cynicism, prevents them from taking any notice. I recently had a woman write to me who'd been to visit the concentration camp at Auschwitz. She'd travelled many thousands of miles to get there and couldn't tell anyone why she felt a need to do so. Once there she experienced a lot of eerie feelings, which, understandably she put down to the atmosphere and history of the place. Then she was compelled to take photographs of some specific buildings, and her photos later revealed what she believed were simple light anomalies.

While she was there, she was drawn to study the groups of photos of the poor inmates of the camps, displayed on the walls. One face in particular stunned her because, not only was she mesmerized by it, but she felt sure she recognized the young man, even though she had obviously never met him as he had died long before she was born into this life. Later in the day a young Polish man came up to her and started speaking to her in Polish. Not only did she understand what he was saying, despite never having learned, heard or spoken Polish in her life, but she was also able to answer him, in Polish! Despite all this she was determined not to believe it could have anything to do with her own past life, perhaps as that young man in the photo, or at least as a friend of his or family member. It seems that her soul angel had a very tough task ahead. And yet, for some reason she also felt compelled to seek me out and write and tell me about it … so maybe there's hope yet.

CHAPTER 5
ANGEL SIGNS

A man on the street is pointing up to the sky. 'Look, an Angel!' he yells. Passersby laugh. 'You fool, that is only a cloud.' How wonderful it would be to see angels where there are only clouds. How sad it would be to see only clouds where there are angels. – **Anonymous**

HOW CAN YOU TELL WHEN AN ANGEL'S AROUND?

As I've said, angels can be very inventive when it comes to signalling their arrival on the scene. White feathers in unexpected places are the top sign, as are unusually coloured feathers. Scents are the second most popular signal – any kind of smell from perfume or burning sage to chocolate. Butterflies and dragonflies are the third sign that most people notice, especially when these appear out of season (as in winter). Then there are rainbows. We all know the scientific reason for them, but we all stand in awe when one appears, and they can be a sign from angels. Other weather changes can be brought about by angels, such as unseasonable snow. I know one woman who found the name of a recently deceased loved one carved in virgin snow with no footprints around it.

Some people sense a gentle draught on the back of their neck when all doors and windows are closed, or a soft touch on their arm when no one's around. Some people feel like they have cobwebs wafting across their faces. Some feel the invisible caress of an angel's wing, or even the feel of wings wrapping themselves right around their body. Some people see images in clouds that mean something to them or make some sense of their current situation. Flowers can sometimes yield unusual properties, such as emitting heat or chill, or dropping their petals in your path. A certain word or phrase might keep being repeated, in a book, in a song, newspaper headlines, hoardings, even in car number plates. You might feel a tingle in a certain part of your body which your angel uses to herald their presence. Or you might see a repetition of the same numbers around you. The most common number used by angels is 11:11, so anything unusual that occurs about that time or on that date, or whenever that number appears, deserves special attention.

An angel will sometimes awaken a person at precisely the same time every night, because they are trying to get that person's attention. Some people hear their name being called, either by an unknown voice or by someone who loves them. It may then be found that no one was actually around to have made the sound. Flickers or sparkles of golden or coloured lights are another good sign – not those that might appear inside your eyes, but those that float independently on the air. The radio or TV might change channels by itself. Objects might disappear and seem lost, only to reappear in a place already searched. You might feel warm, bright sun on your closed eyes on a rainy, cloudy day. Certain birds are used by angels, often white ones, but sometimes it can be crows. Also flocks of birds behaving in strange ways can be seen as a sign of angel manipulation.

CALLING ON ANGELS TO PROTECT YOU

Recently I connected to Jade Goody for her mum, Jackiey, and I was able to tell her that her daughter was saying, 'I'm blowing in the wind.' At that very moment Jackiey was thrilled that an inexplicable breeze blew through the room, lifting the curtains. This was a sign created by Jade but enabled by an angel. People sometimes ask me, 'If I have a sign that appears to come from a passed-over loved one, is it from them, or their angel?' My answer is that the sign has been requested by the loved one, but enabled by their angel. My mum's angel used to let her send me shooting stars whenever I need to know she was still around (shooting stars are another popular sign for many people).

One thing to note is that even if certain objects or events might have a 'rational', natural or scientific explanation, it doesn't always mean that an angel hasn't used them to communicate with us. Rainbows, for instance, are of course a natural event, and yet their appearance at a specific moment can be very meaningful for the person involved. Their angel knows this, and knows they'll get the message, so it's logical that they'd make use of such phenomena. Photographic phenomena can also be explained away scientifically sometimes, but it doesn't mean they aren't valid signs from an angel. Angels will use whatever's available to them to get through to us.

The key to meaningful communication is to open your eyes, while at the same time allowing your right (creative) brain to take over. Your left brain is the side of you that will try to talk you out of belief. You won't get the message if you refuse to accept the messenger. Some people tell me, 'If only I had a physical sign from my angels, then I would believe,' while all the time the signs are all around them, they're just not seeing them.

As you can see, angels will use almost anything to reach us, so remember, the first step towards communicating with your angel is to become aware of your surroundings and notice what is going on around you. Become attentive to anything that seems to stand out from all of the rest of your life.

YOUR CHILD AND ANGEL SIGNS

Children are always more connected spiritually than we are to angels and to the universe in general. It's by observing children that we ourselves can sometimes see how we should think and feel to be more in tune. A visit to Great Ormond Street Hospital for Children would be a real eye-opener for most of us. The children there are by definition very ill for the most part, and the reasons they are having to go through that sort of pain are many and various. One of the most common is that they have contracted, before this life, to change their parents and carers in some way. Such is the love souls have for one another that they are willing to do just that. Their connection to angels is obvious. The children, as one, show extraordinary courage and optimism. Their faces light up with angelic energy at a tiny moment of joy. I had a lady ask me quite vehemently, 'Where was baby P's angel, then?' (Baby P was a very tragic child who died at the hands of his adult carers.) He suffered terribly, and my answer is that we cannot imagine why these things are meant to happen, only that it seems they must, for some reason known only to God and the angels. All I know is that I believe the children are protected by angels, and that the physical suffering they go through is somehow separated from their spirit, left on the surface of their consciousness, while deeper down they are buoyed up on the arms of angels, so that their pain can be endured without destroying their spirit.

Children in general are closer to angels because they live with trust, and naturally take happiness into their hearts in preference to any baser adult emotions such as greed, hatred, revenge – these are emotions that we give them. Adults are very good at instilling fear into their children, which takes away their natural joy. As parents we don't mean to do this, but careless talk about our own fears and dreads rub off on them. I know the world is a tough place and that eventually children have to cope with difficult issues, some sooner than others, but until that time it's our duty to protect their natural attributes, because the longer we can do that the longer they will stay connected. This is why some sick children retain their joy despite their problems – because their parents protect them from the negative aspects of the world for longer, and in so doing give them every chance to stay connected with the angels. This is why children who have been through life-threatening or painful illnesses often grow up to be spiritual adults and great examples to the rest of us.

Children will often talk of a beautiful lady who comes to them in the night, and some will even draw pictures of her. Adults should never ridicule this kind of involvement, even if they do not believe. To do so is to stifle and possibly even destroy a very vital part of their child's spirit. Young children, especially babies who haven't learned to talk yet, will sometimes be found smiling and giggling at something the parents can't see. This is an ability that seems to fade in time, no matter how much it's encouraged, so it should be treasured while it's there.

This is a classic tale of a child's account of seeing an angel. Gennie told me this:

'I was only about 12 years old when I woke up very suddenly in the middle of the night. It was as though someone had jolted me out of sleep, so much that I sat right up. I

*was amazed to see that my room was all shrouded in fog,
as if it was a really misty night and someone had left the
windows open. But it wasn't and they hadn't. I didn't feel at
all scared, which was a bit odd, I later thought. A cloaked
figure appeared out of the mist, standing at the bottom of
the bed. She just radiated love and safety. I believe she was
my angel and to this day, although I never saw her again, I
still feel her around, especially if I'm frightened about something.'*

I recently had a somewhat cynical radio presenter ask me,
'You say that children should be encouraged to be close
to and see angels. Isn't this likely to be scary for them?'
This brings me to the clearest sign of all of the presence of
angels. In my answer to him I said, 'No, because it's not
possible to feel fear in the company of an angel.' So I have
to thank him, because it made me articulate this very vital
point. The way angels make you feel when they are near
totally obliterates the ability to be afraid. You just simply *cannot* be afraid when one is near. The love you feel
from these beings overtakes and surpasses any emotion
you've ever felt before. The one compelling emotion you
feel is safety in any experience whatsoever. So, this feeling
of utter safety, especially if experienced in a less than safe
situation, can mean that angels are near you.

It's nice when I come across other people who are
trying to help children retain their spiritual values. Mimi
Doe is the founder of www.SpiritualParenting.com and

author of five books for parents. She feels, as I do, that the future of the world depends on our children being connected to their spirituality, and to their souls:

'When my daughter Whitney, 4 years old at the time, began telling me about Sophine, an angel who visited her, I had no idea just where this angel would take us. "Mama, Sophine came to my room last night" she told me one morning.

'"Who is Sophine?" I asked, surprised, as my child was not prone to fantasy or make-believe. Whitney was my practical, pragmatic first-born, always reporting in full detail the truth of most any situation.

'"Sophine is the angel who comes to my room each night," she said matter-of-factly.

'Chills ran through my body. I stopped stirring the morning oatmeal and grabbed a piece of paper. It was as if something was telling me that this was important, that I must get it all down exactly as she told me. "Tell me about her, Whitney."

'"Well, I was also an angel before I was born. I watched over you and I picked you to be my mommy. I knew Sophine then, and she comes to me now. I also call her 'One Who Brings Me Flowers'. She makes my flowers grow, Mama. She makes them the colours they are supposed to be."

'I wrote each word down exactly the way she said it. I told her what a blessing it was that she had such a special friend, and how grateful I was that she had picked me to be her mom. She then drew a beautiful picture of Sophine holding

a bunch of flowers with yellow light all around her. The day went on, but I could not keep away from that piece of paper. I believed Whitney. I knew her to be a sensitive and special child, and it seemed incredible, but right, that she would experience an angel.

'A few days later, I was cleaning the house and was about to throw away a shrivelled, sad looking African violet. "Oh no, Mama, don't throw it away," Whitney cried. "Let me put it in my room." Anyone who is a parent knows that sometimes it's easier to comply with our children rather than going into a long song and dance to explain something. I gave the poor plant to Whitney and forgot it.

'The next morning she came running down the stairs with the African violet in her hands. "Look, look, Mama! Sophine made my flower grow. She made it all better." So it was. There were four beautiful little pink violets where only dead stalks existed the day before.

'I had to know if other children experienced angels in the vivid and intimate way my young daughter did. I began asking them. I started with my children's friends and pre-school, kindergarten and first-grade classes in my home town. I would ask the children to tell me about angels, then have them draw pictures of what an angel looked like. The results were breath-taking. In taking the time to listen to and view children's personal visions, I discovered that angels appear to young people in some vivid and non-traditional ways. They aren't always white-winged ladies. They are as rich and varied as the children themselves.

'If so many children saw and experienced angels, I wanted to talk to more who lived much different lives than those close to home. I continued working with children but went out farther than my own community. In an effort to include a wide variety of socio-economic backgrounds, cultures, and religions, I spoke with children across America who described their own angels with candour and conviction. I wanted a way to share children's rich images with the world. My book, Drawing Angels Near, was a result of that desire.

'Sophine, drawn by my daughter that morning four years before, was picked by the editor at my publishers to grace the cover of the book. My editor had no idea when she selected it that it was drawn by Whitney, the inspiration for it all!

'Children do seem to see and experience angels in a vivid and personal way. Validating children's spiritual connection has become my passion. They are still connected with the world so many of us have forgotten. I've given talks and workshops to parents and educators around the world to encourage them to honour and nurture children's divine spirituality – sharing specific tips and techniques to do so. Listening to children's descriptions of angels is certainly a beginning.

'Sophine no longer appears to my daughter, who is now a vibrant college student. It is almost as if she came to manifest these projects for other children and then slipped away from view when Whitney was about 7 or 8. At about 11 years old, however, Whitney quietly shared with me that, "I *have a new angel now, Mama. He was in the kitchen last night and again this morning on the deck with his strong, loving wings around our house."*

'I trust that there are yet more angels surrounding Whitney as she now lives on her own in a college dorm, keeping her safe and lighting her way.'

ANGELIC PROTECTION FOR YOU AND YOURS

It's possible to come under attack from what I call 'psychic vampires' – people who drain you of energy, either intentionally or accidentally. Have you ever picked up your telephone and got a horrible sinking feeling for no real reason when you discover that a certain person is calling? After the call do you feel drained and emotionally exhausted? When you bump into a certain person, do they always stand too close to you, invading your aura and leaving you feeling almost violated? Have you ever found yourself acting totally out of character in a negative way, or suffering sudden loss of memory, or feeling constantly tired despite having plenty of rest? Do you have recurrent nightmares or visions, or a scary feeling that someone is watching you? Is there a room in your house that used to be a haven and yet suddenly feels hostile to you? If you have experienced any of these uncomfortable situations, then you may well be experiencing a 'psychic attack'. There are many methods of calling on your angels to protect you against these kinds of attacks.

Telephone Protection

For the unwelcome psychic vampire on the phone, or the space-invader in person, there are simple means of prevention. For telephone protection, the most obvious is to have a 'caller display' on your phone and ignore calls from that person. The other is to have your feet on the floor and to cross your ankles while talking to them. This helps to ground you and close your body circuit, allowing angelic protection to wrap around you and make you less open to an energy drain. For the person who 'gets in your face' and won't back off, a very simple expedient is to strengthen your own aura by visualizing it all as a bulge in front of you, and then 'pushing' the energy towards the other person. If you persevere with this, they *will* back off, because they won't be able to withstand your angel's power.

Home Protection

To protect your home and all those within it, visualize your house encapsulated in a sparkling globe of white angel light. It might help to liken the shape to that of a snow globe, with your home nestling cosily in the middle of it. Ask your angel to keep this boundary inviolate, even when you're not at home.

Personal Protection

Each morning when you get up, perhaps during your shower, visualize a silver suit. The more sparkly and gaudy you can make the suit, the better it will work, simply because the image will be stronger in your inner eye. See yourself putting on this suit. Do it carefully, seeing each limb going into it – again, the better the visualization the better it will work. Finally, slip the hood over your head and zip the suit up.

During the day you can use another device: if you feel in any way threatened or in danger, imagine inflating the suit, a bit like a car's airbag, in the direction of the threat. For instance if you're a woman alone on a dark street and a man is walking behind you, push the 'bubble' of the inflated suit towards him, and you'll find he'll cross over the road. These actions actually bring your angel's energy into play, and you will be, and feel, safe. You can even visualize dressing each one of your family in a similar suit, if they're not open enough to do so for themselves.

A Visualization for Protection

Every morning, picture a bright white light coming down to your head from your guardian angel. Draw this light over your whole body, holding a piece of rainbow quartz to amplify the protective energy. This takes a bit of practice but it soon becomes second nature. As with anything like this, the key is *intent*. If you see the white light in your mind's eye, it will be there in the form of an energy field that will protect you all day.

This method can be easily tested in a car. When in a moving line of traffic, visualize the light in a bubble over your car, and push it out behind you. You'll find that the car behind will fall back, making you safer physically as well as spiritually.

Safe Place Protection

Another method of visualization is to create a place of safety in your mind. It can be anywhere that you love and can easily picture, like a beach or a walk you love, or it can be a virtual room. Whatever you choose, learn to see an image of this place in every tiny detail. If it's outside, be sure and furnish its image with the sounds you'd normally expect to see there, and make the weather always bright and sunny and cheerful. If it's a virtual room, then see the colours on the walls, which can be rounded to form a sort of nest. Furnish it with huge floor cushions that you can feel cosy sitting on. In any time of threat, just place yourself there and understand completely that nothing but your angel can approach your spirit. It that is your *intent*, then nothing else will be able to.

Power Words Protection

Another way to get protection is to repeat a mantra, giving your angel all the words that mean safety to you. Devise the mantra as one that's easy to remember and say, such as 'I am safe. I am strong. I am untouched.' This will encourage your angel to instruct your subconscious to make it so, and as your higher mind is your most powerful weapon, you will be made safe. Believe it and it will be so.

Group Protection

Any of the above will work for a group, too, but if you meet regularly you should devise your own method of psychic protection. This can also be performed by a family to cleanse their home of dark energy. Everyone should stand in a circle facing the centre, and everyone should join hands to make the circle complete. One elected person should express the purpose of the ritual, such as, 'This group is united in truth and light and is here to share positive thoughts and manifestations. We call on our angels to help us.'

The members should take this as a signal to start visualizing a wall of light around the entire circle. It should then be gradually extended to form a barrier around the entire building they are in. Because this is a joint effort it will be much easier to make the ball of light big enough for this.

After a pre-arranged amount of time, the leader should break the silence by asking the whole group to say a blessing, such as, 'May the divine creator bless this space and all who dwell here. May we all walk in the light of our own truth and remain safe when we leave this place. We thank our angels for their help.'

Bodily Protection

This is to make sure that you haven't created a haven for negativity in your physical body. For this you need to enter a light meditative state, and then concentrate on using your breath to cleanse your body. Ask your angel to impart their strength into your energy. Inhale white light and exhale dark light. Concentrate on how your body is feeling, and keep doing this until you feel an energy shift throughout your system. Then concentrate on each of your chakras in turn, pushing out any blocked energy with expelled air. Search your emotional body for any cords attaching you to negative people or places, and ask your angel to help you cut them.

Spiritual Protection

This is to deny negative influences access into your etheric body. Tune in to your angel and ask them to help you banish any negative energy. See all your bad baggage as rubbish to be thrown out and burnt. Question your higher self as to whether you are opening yourself to psychic attack by hanging on to old resentments or guilt for things you feel you've done wrong. Detach any of these as if they were fishing hooks, snagged into your soul. See the barbs disappear and dissolve, leaving your spirit smooth and untouched.

Emergency Protection

Most religious symbols have the ability to protect their wearer from harm, and this is mainly because the devotee believes in them. They have strong *intent*, and remain safe from harm. If they didn't believe, then the symbols wouldn't work.

Ask your angel to show you a symbol that will work well for you, and see it with your mind's eye. If you suddenly find yourself under attack from psychic forces, you can use the symbol you have chosen and feel close to by 'drawing' it in the air in front of you.

First of all, face the direction from which you feel the attack is coming. 'Draw' the symbol in front of you and then fling your arms out, as if to ward off the danger.

CHAPTER 6
ANGEL COLOURS

And so thy path shall be a track of light, like angels' foot-steps passing through the night. – **words on the wall of a church in Upwaltham, England**

Which colour is best for calling in the angel you need? And if you actually see an angel, what does its colour mean?

That angels have energy which vibrates is fundamental. Everything vibrates in order to exist, including the planet we live on. Angels exist in a higher dimension to us and in order to reach it we have to raise the speed of our vibration. What is not so well known is that certain angel vibrations relate to certain colours and crystals, and that we might get closer to them by utilizing this knowledge. By wearing the right colours or holding a crystal of the right colour, for example, you can gently raise your vibration towards that of your angel.

There are many and varied suggestions as to which colour goes with which angel and how to use that information. You can start by thinking of a purpose for the angel, look up which angel is associated with requests concerning that purpose, and then find out which colours you should concentrate on. The other way to do it is to decide which colour best suits the mood you want to end up with and use that colour to instinctively attract the angel you need. Use whichever method gels best with you. I'll start off by showing you the orthodox list of master path angels and their associated colours, and then move on to what my own experience has taught me.

COLOURS ASSOCIATED WITH ANGELS
Anael
If all the romance has gone from your marriage or relationship, this angel can restore your feelings of love and passion and a need to please your partner. This is also the angel of the environment, so if you want to live a 'greener' life, he can help you find ways to do so. He engenders a love of the planet, so is probably the angel we should all be talking to.

His colours are said to be azure, sea green and lavender.

Asariel
This is the angel who is said to guide our dreams and bring us messages in sleep. He is the angel said to watch over the seas and oceans, so if you're going to be travelling by boat he can protect you. Likewise he can help you manage the deeper areas of your psyche and resolve mental health issues.

His colours are said to be those of the deep oceans, such as navy blue and near black.

Azrael

This is the angel to call on if you are living in fear of death. He can show you that dying is just a transition, whether for you or your loved ones. He can give you the power to be strong for others and is often called upon by those dying to help them be strong for the ones they are to leave behind.

His colours are said to be all shades of dark red.

Cassiel

If you've been trying really hard for promotion and feel you've been treated unfairly, this angel can help. He will give you the strength to persevere, but also redirect you if you're aiming for the wrong target. He's also especially good to talk to about and in gardens, as he can inspire growth.

His colours are said to be those earthy ones such as golden brown, maroon and ginger.

Chamuel

If you're feeling unloved, even by yourself, this angel can comfort you. He'll help you keep negativity at bay and thereby become more attractive to others because everyone likes to be near positive people. If you've had your heart broken, Chamuel will help to mend it and enable you to start to trust in relationships again.

His colours are said to be all shades of pink, from pastel shades right through to rich maroon and burgundy.

Gabriel

If you are afraid for yourself and/or your loved ones, Gabriel is the angel of choice. He will also help you to make tough decisions and, if life throws you a painful situation that can't be avoided, this angel will walk next to you through the darkness.

His colours are said to be purest snow white and gleaming gold.

Jophiel

If you're puzzled by your life, this angel can bring answers to questions. He is also the one to call on if you're lacking in inspiration, for instance if you are a writer suffering from writer's block. He will also help if you're about to take a driving test or exams.

His colours are said to be primrose and lemon.

Michael

Known to be the warrior, Michael helps people show courage in difficult or dangerous situations. He can also wield his sword when asked to separate you from people you know are harming you but still feel tied to. He'll also help you complete tasks that you feel are beyond your capabilities.

His colours are said to be petrel blue and aquamarine or turquoise.

Raphael

If you're having problems with a relationship, and yet you're sure it's worth saving, call on Raphael to help you find the right words to heal the situation. Raphael will also help if you need to think creatively and are finding that difficult to do. He can bring you visions that will clear the mists of confusion away.

His colours are said to be lime green and leaf green.

Sammael

If you're feeling lacklustre and not up to some challenge you're about to face, this angel can rekindle your passion for the job in hand and the strength of energy to keep going. This is the angel said to help soldiers in battle, not to fight, but to survive. I would say this is the angel that I've spoken of appearing to soldiers in the trenches and saving their lives.

His colour is said to be red.

Uriel

This angel is said to help you if you have a lot of conflict in your life, especially if it's self-inflicted. Many people try to live in the past or in the future instead of the present; Uriel can bring you back to the moment. The angel of passion, he can also give you the determination to bring purpose to your life.

His colours are said to be all those of fire, such as red, yellow and orange.

Zadkiel

This is the angel to call on specifically if you have gone through a lot of negative events and have been left sullied by them. He will cleanse your spirit and protect you from the same thing happening in the future. He will help you to forgive others and thereby free yourself of the past.

His colours are said to be lilac, violet and silver.

MY OWN EXPERIENCE OF ANGEL COLOURS

These are the colours I've come to associate with certain angel messages and vibrations through personal experience. These colours will work powerfully for you whether you wear clothes of these colours or carry them with you in crystal form.

- Blue (suggested crystal – labradorite): *When aspiring to a higher purpose, and needing an angel dedicated to this endeavour, the brighter shades of blue such as royal blue will help you attune to the right angel help.*

- Red (suggested crystal – ruby is the obvious, but a less expensive alternative would be garnet or red jasper): *When needing courage to face adversity, such as a surgical procedure or to achieve something that you are frightened of, such as speaking in public or visiting the dentist, wearing red will bring in the right angel energy.*

- Gold (suggested crystal – any gold jewellery):
  *Gold, as you might expect, can bring abundance
  through angel intervention. This can be financial
  or it can be emotional wealth you're seeking. By
  wearing gold you'll help yourself create the right
  vibrational energy to draw in the right angel.*

- Yellow (suggested crystal – lemon quartz, or for
  bright yellow – amber): *When this is a gentle pastel
  colour, wearing it can also make your energy gentle
  and sensitive. So if you're about to try and diffuse a
  conflict between, say, two family members who are
  feuding, this will bring in the right angelic help.
  If it's a bright daffodil yellow, then you're literally
  looking for some sunshine or good news in your life.*

- White (suggested crystal – moonstone): *The
  colour of the pure at heart, white obviously attracts
  all kinds of angels. It's particularly useful if you're
  looking for guidance out of a knotty problem, or are
  at a crossroads of some kind.*

- Lilac (suggested crystal – pale amethyst): *The
  colour of psychic energy. This is the one to wear if
  you need angelic help in developing any kind of
  psychic ability.*

- Turquoise (suggested crystal – turquoise): *If you're
  hoping or need to travel, especially across oceans, but
  can't find the means to achieve this, this colour will
  help draw in the right angel to help you.*

- Purple (suggested crystal – deep amethyst): *Traditionally the colour worn by royalty and people of importance, wearing this colour will help you to get angels to increase your self-confidence. If someone's been putting you down and making you feel small, this colour with bring angelic chutzpah to help!*

- Pink (suggested crystal – rose quartz): *You might be feeling alone and unloved and have no one to call on. Wear and carry pink and your angel will be happy to arrive laden with love and an ability to help you love yourself.*

- Green (suggested crystal – peridot or fluorite): *Always the colour of healing, it's the one to wear when the doctors of this world can't help and you need some divine intervention to get your health back on track. You might simply receive healing or you might be guided towards some alternative practitioner who can help you.*

- Black (suggested crystal – black onyx): *If you have a situation coming up when you'll need to wear your 'grown-up' head and take things very seriously in order to succeed, this sombre colour will help bring in an angel that will nurture those traits in you.*

- Silver (suggested crystal – anything made of silver or rainbow quartz): *If you're feeling a need for heavenly protection, perhaps from a jealous person, or if you think you are under psychic attack from someone, silver, the colour of a sword, is the colour to wear or have with you to get that help.*

- Brown (suggested crystal – brown topaz): *You might be facing a situation that you'd rather back out of, something that's going to require hands-on action you'd rather not contemplate. This colour will bring in an angel that will give you the courage you need to walk into the event with confidence in your ability to do and say the right thing.*

- Grey (suggested crystal – hematite): *If matters around you need some clarity and the future looks cloudy and uncertain, then wear or carry grey, the colour of the ancient high-priests' heart stones, and help will be forthcoming that will show you the way out of the maze.*

- Burgundy (suggested crystal – chronos): *The colour of nature, this would be the one to wear if you feel a need for an angel that is naturally attuned to the earth. Perhaps you've found yourself lacking in grounding and need a spiritual tether.*

- Orange (suggested crystal – carnelian): *The colour to wear to receive angelic help in the home. If you feel that perhaps your house is not quite the cosy nest your family needs, wearing this colour will help.*

In the angel portraits I do, I also use the colours that appear in them to give the sitter a reading. These colours combine to provide different meanings to those above, and the meanings also depend on where the colours appear, whether in the gown or wings for instance. In angel gowns, a gold combined with red would usually signify karmic or past-life importance, and with the addition of turquoise this could mean a need to travel to a place from a past life in order to resolve a problem. However, if green were added to the red and gold, then that would signify that past-life healing is needed.

Red and blue, on the other hand, in most cases would signify a need to be strong and honest in a difficult situation. When these colours are in the wings it can signify events that involve the above but are naturally going to happen, without intervention. These types of readings can be very complicated, though, and there is no definitive chart of the various colours and their meanings.

There follow just a few examples of the messages the angels bring to me through these portraits.

A Many-coloured Angel

'There are many colours in your angel, and it looks a little chaotic – this is a reflection, a mirror of your energy (or aura). Her wings, while having a lot of gold (a sign of a very bright future) also have missing parts. There are lots of half-formed events around her. Most of your problems stem from this chaotic atmosphere you carry around with you. Difficulty in sleeping, and the inability to stop talking at the right time, are all due to the same thing. You really need to develop the ability to shut your mind off. This requires *huge patience and practice for someone like you, who is naturally a 'high-energy' personality. What you need to do is to channel this energy in the right direction – so that you can use it when you need to and not waste it when you don't.*

'You require much more time than most to ready your mind for relaxation and sleep, so you should not have your mind stimulated in any way for an hour before you go to bed. It would be a good idea to buy a nice meditation CD and play that while you go to sleep. You are a very curious person, with intelligent (if frequently unnecessary) thoughts, and spiritually you need to find a definite path – a definite goal, rather than dabbling, which you tend to do.

'Sometimes you are full of optimism and other times full of doubt. You have to bring structure and peace to that formidable energy of yours in order that the future which is meant to be can reveal itself clearly in front of you.

'So we see a clear pattern here. Imagine you are like a little hot air balloon floating on high. All around on the horizon are those events you so long to have happen. They are just waiting there to come to you, all their shapes carved into white, fluffy clouds.

But meanwhile, the air currents around your balloon are turbulent. You can see how this would make it impossible for the events to reach you. The more you thrash around and try to make them arrive, the more you push them away by making the wind gust and billow.

'Learn to be calm and the air will calm, and things will start to arrive.

'You are right that you have some big and exciting things to do, and they will come, but you have to relax.

'Energy is magnetic – that is, what you project is what you will get. If you project excited, expectant energy, that's what you will get back – excited expectation, with nothing completely forming, a sort of kaleidoscope, constantly changing, with nothing clear. If you can project calm expectant energy, you will get completely formed events that won't be clouded and disrupted by your constantly moving energy.

'This is what will happen then:

- You will be balanced, which will be good for your health, too.

- You will meet a new person, who will be very influential in your life.

- He will be a foreigner, and his first language will not be English.

- You will quickly recognize that this is the one you have been waiting for to lead you.

- You will start a business together.

- You will move to an island.

- You will learn to hear your angels for yourself.

- You will learn a 'touch' form of healing.

- You will travel the world.

'All this can happen so long as you are ready. Try and imagine that when your mind is too busy, it's like a pool of water with a tendril of dye in it. If you swirl the water the dye will disperse and never coalesce into a definite colour. This is what your angel is clearly concerned about. Many times she has tried to direct you, but has been unable to maintain the connection.

'If there are some meditation classes near to you, you should enrol so that you can learn the necessary techniques to be able to switch off completely. This will also raise your vibration, which will facilitate communication.'

Wings of Connection

'You'll notice that your angel's wings are different from each other. One has vibrant "peacock" colours, the other is pink and lilac. This means that your gifts will be a combination of psychic (intuitive) energy and the product of a creative mind. All you have to watch is to keep the balance right. Your path is very well-defined, so you need to measure each new step before you take it. Materialism can never be allowed to take over, or your inspiration might fade.

'You've had a very pivotal event in your spiritual life that was a bit like dropping a pebble into a pond. The ripples are ever spreading outwards. This event has changed the way you see the world and, most importantly, the way the world sees you.

'There is someone watching over you. In fact there are two people watching over you, which is great news. One in particular was someone you would have trusted with your life. Another impor-

tant aspect in your life is that what you do should be in balance with nature. You're very much the sort of person who could work and live mostly in a city, but would appreciate a country cottage in the middle of nowhere with no mobile phone signal! 'At this moment in time the most vital thing for you is "connections" – as above, so below. In other words, you must continue always to find time to meditate, because those "above" are using this time to set these connections in place. We often spend our lives banging our heads against brick walls or closed doors. So far, you have managed to spot that "open window" you're being directed to, and other people might look at you and think, "Isn't she lucky?" They might even tell you that you're lucky to your face. No such thing. You are obeying the rules of synchronicity and that is making your own luck. 'I hope you like your angel. She is very beautiful and, although I haven't seen a photo of you, you must be, too, because your angel is what I call a "mirror angel". In other words, she is a reflection of what your soul looks like.'

Globe of Anguish

'You can see the pinkish, harsh-looking globe that is sort of spoiling the flow of this otherwise beautiful picture. This represents the damage your quarrel with your daughter is doing to your energy and your soul's progress. The raggedness of the globe shows the bad place your daughter is in right now, and, sadly, given past-life issues and her current state of mind, this is something only you can change (but you already knew that, didn't you?)

'The remark she made to you, about you, is actually something in her subconscious from a past life you spent together. Families often come back together time after time, trying to put right what once went wrong, and often failing. It then gets ever more complicated until it's virtually impossible to sort out. If you let this go on, then in the next life you'll both have even more problems to remedy, and it will be even more difficult than it is now.

'Your angel is not suggesting that you try to tell your daughter about past-life issues, as she won't accept this. If you can, what you need to do is put what she said out of your mind. Forgive her if you will, for she has no idea why she said that, and most importantly it is not relevant and only damaging to your relationship in this life.

'Because you now know why she said it, your angel hopes you can let go of the hurt and consign that, too, to your past life. In time these things will come forward again to be healed, but for now the important thing is not to let things get worse, which they will do with inaction.

'You have to be able to interact with your grandchildren, and if you can understand that your daughter is stuck right now, and that only you can help her, you should be able to put her attitudes to one side.

'If you can arrange a meeting, even if by "accident", then with the knowledge that your angel has given you, you should be able to draw some of that golden energy in and use it as a buffer between you and any hurt. Your daughter does not have the knowledge and, right now, she's angry *(but doesn't know why), hurt and nonplussed as to how to get over these issues. With the right energy you should simply be able to rise above it and act in a totally benevolent way, with your eye and your heart firmly fixed on the 'end game'. That way you will win, and eventually so will your daughter.*

'With your career, all that gold also signifies the obvious: financial gain. There is a new investor on the cards, someone who will have great marketing skills. A new market for the business. You can't go on as you are, but with this new injection of cash and expertise, things will improve. There will be ups and downs, but you should hang in there.

'Relationship is tied to career, so isn't this interesting ... new guidance, new places across the sea, some fear, but yes, a happy ending. It seems to me that you should share your business interests with this soul, who is destined to be a partner in more ways than one. As always this will require great trust, something you don't find easy.'

SENSING ANGEL COLOUR

If you progress far enough to sense an angel presence around you, but don't know which angel it is or what they might be trying to tell you, there is yet another way forward. Calm your breathing, open your mind and sense a colour, the first that comes to mind. Once you have a colour you can read all of the above and come to a conclusion as to which angel it might be and, from there, what they might be trying to communicate with you about.

Even if you haven't progressed that far, simply calming your mind and letting a colour form in it can help you to draw the angel you need closer to you quite naturally. This form of colour meditation can be very effective, because simply by filling your mind with a certain colour and nothing else, you can lower the speed of your brainwaves, and thereby raise the speed of your energetic vibration, closer to that of the angels.

CHAPTER 7
DREAM ANGELS

As to prophecy and good fortune: angels can only speak of it – only humans can manifest it. – **Anonymous**

If angels come to you in dreams, what do the dreams mean?

Dreams are a good place to interact with angels, for once we're in a sleep state our minds are very much more open to angelic energy. The dream state is also one of the best times to connect with our own spirituality, with none of the constrictions placed on us by society during our waking lives. Dreams are a particularly convenient and easy way for angels to speak to us. That's because our brain waves in deep dream state are alpha frequency. This is the same state of mind you might have when you're awake and have a sudden moment of inspiration. You know that time when you've been searching for an answer to a problem and it suddenly comes to you in a flash? So in REM (the dream state) your brain is in the heightened state, whereas your body is still and can even be paralysed. This is the state of mind best for actually reprogramming your subconscious mind, too, so it's no surprise that it's at this time that we can get messages from our angels.

The basis for these messages, however, the time when we actually take a step into the angel's dimension, happens well before we reach REM sleep. It happens when we're just at the point of deep (but as yet dreamless) sleep. It's at this point that our brain waves are at their slowest, the delta frequency. This is the same state we can reach by undergoing something deeply relaxing, such as sound therapy or deep meditation. And the reason this helps our brain state get closer to the angels is because the slower our brain waves, the higher our vibrational speed.

To encourage this kind of communication, try meditating yourself to sleep. A good CD can help you with this. You'll fall asleep very naturally and also you'll have banished your everyday cares, which will work in two ways. First, you'll have paved the way for pure angelic communication, and also you'll have raised your vibration to a point where you can reach them. Don't worry about specifically asking for any particular messages, just leave yourself open to your angels entering your dreams and telling you what you need to know, rather than what you think you want to know.

Other ways to achieve this kind of sleep state are either to count slowly backwards with each slow, outgoing breath, or visualize a story in your mind, something like one of the meditations in *Angel Whispers*. This should work very well.

REPETITIVE, REALISTIC DREAMS

Soul angels are the most common ones to bring us dreams. If you have dreams or nightmares that repeat over time and don't seem to be related to your current life and the people you know, then the odds are very high that you're being given a past-life nudge. As soon as you wake up from this type of dream, perhaps featuring people wearing odd clothing that doesn't seem to fit today, or in which you were taken to a place somewhere you've never been and yet feels very true, write down notes for future reference. If you take no notice, then eventually these dreams will become more sinister, turning into nightmares as your soul angel becomes more desperate for you to realize what it is you're being shown.

WHAT'S THE DIFFERENCE BETWEEN NORMAL DREAMS AND PAST-LIFE VISIONS?

One way to tell the difference between ordinary dreams and past-life recall is that with a dream, or a nightmare, no matter how scary or upsetting it is, once you're awake its effects will quickly fade away. With past-life recall, the high emotions you feel during the dream will be rekindled whenever you think about the events in the dream, even when you're awake, and even weeks or months later. Past-life emotions endure.

Also, past-life visions always feature clothes that match the period you're dreaming of. Ordinary dreams, except those classic Freudian ones where you find yourself in a state of undress in public, don't usually feature much about clothes. Because past-life visions are actually memories rather than just dreams about events in your current life, or the current day, they can provide you with a great deal of detail about that life, especially when it comes to authentic smells, sights or clothing. In past-life dreams you'll also encounter a lot of people you don't know in this life, yet have intimate information about, and of course you'll find yourself in strange places you've never visited and yet seem to have detailed knowledge of.

WHAT DO PAST-LIFE VISIONS MEAN?

The most common reason for past-life dreams is that your soul angel is trying to tune you in to your own soul, and through that for you to realize your purpose for being here in this life at this time. If you're unable to get a fix on your past lives alone, you'll need to go for past-life therapy. Tuning in to your past lives is the most successful way to remember your life's purpose. There is a very comprehensive list of such therapists on my website.

DREAMS THAT FEATURE ANGELS

If you actually see angels in your dreams, then there is almost always a message included that relates to your higher self. The most likely cause is that for some reason you're not connecting enough with that part of yourself in your waking state. Dream-state feels safer; you don't have to really commit yourself the way you do in your day-to-day life.

Quite often having dreams that feature angels can mean that perhaps you don't stand in your own truth while you're awake. In other words, you aren't prepared to stand up for your beliefs for fear of ridicule. This is something that you have to come to terms with. Getting back to the innocent trust that you had when you were a child, that gift you had of simply speaking the truth, can require a lot of courage in this day and age, where anything out of the common consciousness is pounced on and used as an excuse for abuse.

DREAMS THAT FEATURE PASSED-OVER LOVED ONES

To me these are some of the most beautiful gifts from our angels. It is very common for people to receive messages of reassurance about their loved ones in an angel-inspired dream. One of the most interesting and convincing aspects of these dreams is that often several members of the family will experience the exact same dream. When my sister Janet died many years ago, my other sister and I had the same dream. We were all three of us at a sort of party, and were all dressed very prettily. My other sister and I both approached Janet separately in the dream and were told the same thing: 'Stop worrying about me! Look, I'm fine. You can see I'm having a great time!'

Recently at a workshop another woman told me of her dream about her lost child. The child was brought to her by a young man with long, wavy hair, who told her that he was watching over her son until they were reunited.

ANGEL-INSPIRED DREAMS AND THEIR MEANINGS

Flying

If your angel takes you flying in your dream, this will usually be at a time in your life when you're contemplating some big life crossroads. Perhaps you want to set up in business and wonder if it will be a success. If you fly successfully in the dream, then your angel is telling you that your venture will be a success, too. So many times in life people are afraid to let their hopes take flight in case they fail. This sort of dream can give you a clear message about whether you should proceed.

Fleeing

If your dream features you running away from someone, or even chasing someone else, this can be your angel's way of helping you address your fears. This kind of dream means you should face up to them and be honest about what you're afraid of. You might even find yourself running from yourself. In this case you really aren't being honest with yourself and you need to think long and hard about what you really want to achieve and whether you can do it in your current fearful state of mind. However, of course, if you're running from hunters of another era, then this could be a past-life vision.

Houses

If you constantly dream of living in different houses, then this can mean your angel is trying to tell you that there are many more facets to you yet to be discovered. If this is the case then you owe it to yourself to have the courage to stretch yourself in any area that previously has daunted you, such as relationships, work or your social life.

Lucid Dreams

This sort of dream gives you control over it. You become aware that you're writing the script of the dream as you go along, and can influence the action with your thoughts. This is a great dream to have because it means that your angel is telling you that you do have the power to create your own reality and you should translate your faith in yourself into your waking life.

Dreams Featuring Spirit Guides

If you think you're being introduced to your guide in a dream, then this is exactly what's happening. Take this dream at face value. Sometimes if our waking minds aren't open or calm enough for this to happen, your angel will bring your guide directly to your subconscious mind through a dream state.

Journeys

If you dream of a long, sometimes difficult journey where you have to keep seeking help, this is your angel telling you that throughout your life you will need angelic help and you shouldn't be concerned about having to ask for it. They are there to help.

Astral Travel

The official definition of this phenomenon is: an esoteric interpretation of any form of out-of-body experience that assumes the existence of an 'astral body' (i.e. one that is separate from the physical body and capable of travelling outside it). Astral projection, or travel, indicates that the astral body leaves the physical body in order to travel in the astral plane (a place of alternative existence). Angels are quite capable of using this experience to make a point or demonstrate the mysterious elements of our being to us.

Andrew sent me this:

'One night after going to sleep, I suddenly found myself at a friend's house in America. At first I thought I was dreaming, but then I slowly realized that some of the people there didn't seem to be able to see me. I was invisible! I walked around the dining room, where a dinner party was going on. People had finished their meal and were moving to sit in the more comfortable chairs around the room. I sat down, too, but almost immediately someone sat on top of me! It didn't hurt, though – I couldn't feel their weight, and it seemed that they obviously couldn't feel me underneath them. I was able to stand up again without disturbing the person. Some people, just a few, could see me and they spoke to me, but strangely and vaguely, as if they were the ones in a dream. It became obvious to me that it wasn't a dream. I was astral travelling!

'I'd never been in my friend's dining room before, so I looked around in interest. I noted the big oval polished table and the wooden panelling around the walls. I was particularly interested to see an item I had sent my friend as a gift, on one of the shelves that lined one wall. Eventually I decided to go outside and, just like that, there I was. I could see all the parked cars and just wandered around. I walked down to the electronic gate at the entrance, then I started to feel tired and felt myself being pulled away. I felt as if I was on a piece of elastic, and it was gently flexing, making me feel drawn to go with it. Before I knew it I was flying at speed over land, and then the ocean, so fast that everything was a blur. Then I suddenly pinged back into my body, where it waited on my bed in England. I was wide awake immediately and I could remember every detail.

'The next day I emailed my friend and described it all to him. He emailed back to say it had all happened exactly as I'd seen: the furniture, the party, the people, everything – even down to my gift on the shelf. It was an incredible experience and I can't wait for the next one. I think I often travel out of my body, but don't always remember it. What this all proves to me is that we do live in a quantum universe, where everything and every place is accessible to everyone on a spiritual level. I think everyone can go out of their body if they really want to, or maybe we all travel round like that at night but just don't remember it when we wake up. I think what happened to me that night was actually "remote viewing", and I think it was the same kind *of thing that I read about the government using to spy on people in the 1960s. I believe there is a lot of secret research done into it, right up to today.'*

From Graham comes this story:

'Back when I was about 20, I was living and working in Cambridge. One night I went to bed as usual in my bedsit room, but I didn't go to sleep right away. I was just drifting, the way you do, on the verge of sleep but not quite getting there. Just when I was about to go to sleep, I felt a floating sensation and I seemed unusually relaxed, as if I was resting on something so soft that I couldn't feel it. Then suddenly my nose bumped into something. I opened my eyes and was astonished to see the ceiling right in front of me. I was just hanging in mid-air. Although my nose had physically felt bumping into the ceiling, I knew that I must in fact be out of my body; otherwise I would have been defying gravity!

'Surprisingly, I wasn't at all scared by the prospect that I had left my physical body. What was frightening, though, was that it felt so normal, as if I had done this many times before. This meant that probably my spirit had been flying around without me knowing about it consciously – who knows where I'd been, or what I'd been doing?! Now that was terrifying!

'I stayed calm, though, and simply willed myself back into my body. I went back so fast that I never felt any sensation – I was just suddenly back, lying in bed looking up at

the ceiling. My immediate reaction was that I must have imagined it, but I could still feel the absolutely real touch of the ceiling on my nose, and I knew it had been a genuine out-of-body experience.

'Back then I wasn't really into spiritual stuff and so I never tried to do it again, right up to the current day, although given how familiar it felt, it's possible I've done it lots of times and just not remembered.'

Both Andrew and Graham were taken on little out-of-body trips by their angels, and I think it's safe to say they were both changed by them!

NDE – NEAR DEATH EXPERIENCE

Sometimes angels bring us back from the brink of death because we get there when we weren't meant to. Here are some examples.

Sue writes:

'Back in the late 1960s I was suffering from a very bad Asian flu virus that was going around. Feeling rotten, I decided a hot bath might do the trick, but once in there I felt even worse: dizzy and disorientated. I managed to get out and the next thing I knew I was travelling along a dark tunnel. Coming towards me was this very beautiful and very bright light. It was so full of the most amazing love that it was very tempting to just keep going. I could hear my sister calling me from the light. (My sister had

tragically passed away a few years previously.) But I saw a golden being barring the way and somehow I knew it was not my time yet, so I called to my sister that I had to go back. I turned laboriously around and fought my way back along the tunnel and into my body, which felt like wading through hot jelly. It was very difficult to get back. I could hear my husband calling my name as he tried to rouse me. I was lying in a heap on the bathroom floor and he had been trying to get me to wake up. He was very relieved when I regained consciousness.

'Although this is now 35 years or so on, the memory is still as fresh as when it happened. I was left with the knowledge that we are deeply and unconditionally loved. The explanation that this was just my brain closing down does not wash with me, because in this life I have never experienced such a radiant light or such deep, amazing love.

'I had such a sense of homecoming during the experience that it made me convinced that we come from the light and return to it when we die. My religious upbringing had taught me that there is no death, but had not given me any preconceived ideas of the tunnel and the light. Much later I read a book on the subject, and it was wonderful to find so many others who'd had the same experience. I've always been a believer, but at the same time I've always been uncomfortable with organized religion. So much of the church message seems to be about fear, whereas I found out that we are deeply and unconditionally loved. Did the experience stop me from making the usual human errors? Not a bit

of it, I jumped right in and made all the usual mistakes, with the certain knowledge that I was nonetheless loved, and that life is for living to the full, picking yourself up off the ground when you fall, and diving straight back in.'

It's clear that Sue's time had not come yet, and her angel made sure she went back to where she was meant to be!

Glauco told me this story, which as well as demonstrating an NDE also confirms that children are very spiritually attuned:

'When I was 8 my father took me and my two brothers fishing in a river called Rio Guaiba in Porto Alegre, Brazil. It was a hot day and very sunny. When we got there my father was setting up camp when we ask him if we could walk upriver a little bit.

'At first he said no, but after we begged a little bit he agreed, but told us not to go in the water. He said that a few times.

'We started to walk near the water and we got to this bush that was half on the land and half in the water. I don't remember which one of us had the idea to go by it in the water, grabbing the bush to get to the other side. My brother Marco, aged 10, went first. He took a few steps and somehow he lost his footing. He went under, then my older brother Carlon tried to help him and went under also. I don't know why but I went after them. None of us could swim.

'I started to panic. I was really scared. I remember trying to breathe but I couldn't, water was going in instead of air. I remember moving my arms and legs frantically, trying to save my life. I remember my body hitting things under the water. I don't know what I was hitting but it was painful. That day the river was moving fast from west to east towards the ocean. I don't know how much time went by, but after a while I couldn't move any more. I remember just floating under water and I hit bottom. The water was brown and I couldn't see anything. I knew I was dying and I screamed, "Please God help me!" I don't know how but I knew that God was the only one that could help me.

'That was when I felt my life fading, and then I heard the most pleasing voice telling me to relax and that everything was going to be OK. I then felt arms embracing me. I knew it was a male and that he was very kind and gentle. I was so happy and confused at the same time. We were floating in mid-air. I then realized that I was not dead, not yet anyway. I sensed we were going up very fast. All my pains were gone and I could breathe again. My body was not solid anymore, I could see right through it, but I could still feel me.

'Then I saw that we were going towards this light, slowly at first. When we got close to the light, it just engulfed me. It was brighter than the sun but didn't hurt my eyes. The angel that was with me said "Tchau" and faded away. I was floating there for a moment thinking, "What's happening?" I felt connected to everything and that everything *was connected to me. Then I felt I was not alone anymore. I could see this shape of a man coming closer. When he got close enough, I felt the most beautiful feeling of love and belonging. There are no words my human mind can use to describe this feeling. Imagine yourself in an airplane and the airplane blows up! Then you wake up (it was just a dream). Kind of like that. I was so happy I wasn't dead for real, but where was I? (That place felt more real than this one.)*

'This angel (I call them angels) came closer to my right side and spoke to me, but his lips were not moving. He was talking to my mind. I could hear him through mind, being, and my soul. He told me he was there to help me with my questions (and boy, did I have questions) but first he started to show me my life like a movie. My life was going backwards. I remember thinking, "How bad can this be, I'm only 8 years old?" The first image I saw was something bad that I did (I used a key to scratch a car). I could feel the pain that I caused because of my actions. Then I remember thinking, "Oooh no! I'm in trouble!" My angel surprised me by saying, "Don't worry, these are just lessons." I remember thinking, "Oh crap, he can read my mind, too." He heard that too and gave me this lovely, beautiful smile. This movie was showing, second by second, my entire life and everything I saw I could feel the results of. Like, everything I did had a life of its own. He showed me the things I did out of love, too. He showed me the time I befriended this homeless boy. I took him home with me. We showered together. We

ate together and I gave him some of my clothes, too. I could feel how happy I made my angel feel. He told me that those are the things that really matter, those were the things that will make a difference in the world for the better.

'As my life was going backwards I saw me as a baby inside my mother, then just a molecule of life, really, really small but alive. Then the movie stopped and he said two words, and everything I wanted to know was answered by it. All my questions were answered in an instant. Then I started to miss my life as I knew it. I started to think about my mother and I could feel how her pain would be when she heard the news that all her sons had died. I knew my angel was showing me this because it wasn't my time, my mission wasn't done. What mission? I still don't know. I don't know how long all of this took, as I didn't have the sense of time anymore. Anyway, I was missing my life and I wanted to go back. I had flashbacks about playing soccer with my friend, being hugged by my mom, the sun, the rain, things that made me happy. I also knew my angel did this for a reason, because any sane person would not want to go back.

'I also realized for the first time how beautiful and fragile Earth really is. I could sense the Earth breathing like it was alive. I could see a light around everything that was alive, trees, flowers, grass, animals, volcanoes and humans. I sensed that humans are in control over other living things. I've had the word (aura) stamped in my mind ever since.

'Then I felt a jolt in my soul, a feeling that I was back in my body. Next thing I knew I was being held by another

angel. He was pushing me out of the water. It was then that I realized that I was human again. Oh my God, what a feeling! I wish I could make everyone feel that feeling.

'*Then I felt like I was drunk. I saw this beautiful blue sky and I could breathe again. Then I thought, "Where are my brothers?" I looked to my right and there they were, walking out of the water with me! Oh my God! Thank you! Thank you! Thank you! I have tears in my eyes now thinking about it. Then I saw people rushing towards us, some were crying, some were smiling and hugging each other. They felt as happy as I did! Why? Then this police officer was talking on his radio; he said, "I found them, I found the kids!" People were amazed, "This can't be them! They couldn't survive 22 minutes under water!" I was trying to tell them what happened but I couldn't speak.*

'*I still have a little stutter today but I don't care about that. I don't know which is better, being back here or having the knowledge that we never die. Today, I take things as they come and I try to do everything with love. But that sometimes is really hard because we live in a world of uncertainty. People don't know who God really is. They make it really hard for me to love them as I should, but I forgive them and love them on the inside, even though I don't show them sometimes. God knows what I mean.*

'*My brothers and I never talked about this til Christmas of 2007 (38 years later). I asked Marco if he remembered anything. He told me that an angel asked him not talk about it. A week went by and I asked Carlon what hap-*

pened. He said that we died and that an angel saved us. He said he also saw the movie. I don't know why but we never get too deep into this conversation. I think we are scared that something will happen, because we were asked not to talk about it. As I get older I have the urge to tell the world that God and heaven are very real. I have to be very responsible when talking about this. I don't feel that I am the one writing this, but my soul. I pray that one day the human race, the sons and daughters of God, will live on Earth with that love and peace that I felt, and come to the realization that we are one.'

I love Glauco's story and I'm very grateful that he was willing to share it. How great would it be if everyone grew up with the knowledge that this young man had? The world would certainly be a better place. Who knows what incredible things Glauco is destined to do in this lifetime?

CHAPTER 8
CUPID'S ANGELS

To love for the sake of being loved is human, but to love for the sake of loving is angelic. – **Alphonse de Lamartine**

Can angels help you with your relationships? How can you get some angelic help to find Mr or Ms Right, or sort out your family feuds?

CHOOSING YOUR PARTNER WITH ANGELIC HELP

Wouldn't it be good if you could use angels to help you choose the perfect partner without ever having to say a word, enter the hunt, take a risk or even worry about your own appearance? Imagine being able to choose a man or woman from a distance and know that he or she will suit you.

Well, you *can* do this. Through the vortex of your guardian angel's energy you can become able to see other people's auras. If you use your angels to help you find someone with a compatible aura to yours, it's almost guaranteed that they'll make you a very good partner.

Your angels can help you develop the gift of seeing and interpreting auras using the list that I have channelled through from my own angels, below.

What are auras? As humans we are creatures of electrical impulses, and like any other electrical device we create an energy field around us. This is an aura. Our auras emanate from our chakras. Chakra means 'wheel' in Sanskrit, and the body has several spinning energy centres that resemble spinning wheels. These chakras, or energy centres, regulate the flow of energy through our spiritual system. There are seven chakras: the crown, brow (or third eye), throat, heart, solar plexus, centre and root, all creating colours in our energy fields.

If you've ever met somebody new, and straight away felt like backing away from them, it could well be that your auras are not compatible. Similarly, instant attraction and a feeling of comfort when someone comes into your personal space means that your auras are in balance with each other.

To use auras to select a partner, you have to ask your angel to let you see them and interpret them. Some very lucky people are born with the natural ability to see auras. These people are, of course, in tune with their angels, and are quite rare. Most of us have to learn how to do this.

To start, sit relaxed in a chair next to a plain and preferably quite light-coloured wall. Close your eyes and ask your angel to help you with this task. Breathe evenly, slowly, and put all your cares and agendas out of the way. When you feel your angel is near, from the tingle you get, the scent or whatever sign your angel uses, open your eyes slowly. Don't lose the rhythm of your breathing and focus only on your angel's energy around you. Breathe with your eyes – that is, instead of using your normal vision sense, instead of seeing and interpreting everything around you, just see in a totally focused way a spot just in front of you, and nothing peripheral. Don't let anything else interrupt your sight. Raise one hand, level with your eyes, with the fingers splayed. Stare at your fingertips but let your eyes go 'soft' so that they start to concentrate on the air just above your fingers. With a little patience you will start to see a fuzzy outline around the tips of your fingers, almost like a double image. They might also resemble the air disturbance seen around a fast-moving vehicle, or a mirage in the desert.

Once you can see this, move your hand slowly from side to side. You'll see that the image follows and moves with them. Now you should be able to see that the outline goes down between your fingers, too. The harder and longer you stare, the more clear this aura will become.

After a while you'll notice that the outline flares at the top, and starts to look more like tendrils of smoke than an outline with a sharp edge. Now place your hands, palms together, in front of you, focus on the aura between them, and then slowly draw them apart. As your hands move further apart, the two auras of your hands will separate. By now you'll probably wonder how you never saw auras before, and if you try you'll now be able to see them around everything, even trees and rocks.

The next thing you need to do is to start seeing colours. This takes nothing more than practice, practice, and practice. You need to get some friends to act as guinea pigs for you. I've yet to meet anyone who isn't immediately interested and willing when you ask, 'Can I look at your aura?' Colours will come gradually, starting with one or two until you can build the whole shape of the person in wavy blocks of colours.

Before you start using your newfound skill, you need to know what the colours mean:

- Blue/Green: A healer who can soothe your troubled soul, but might be bland and dull

- Black: A troubled soul themselves, who could be very needy and demanding

- Pastel blue: Will endorse your emotions and be a tender and considerate lover; can be lacking in ambition

- Sky blue: A natural person who cares for the world, but might not have enough time to give you attention

- Petrel blue: Intuitive, and will always know what you are thinking, which means he or she will know if you lie!

- Royal blue: A decisive person who knows where he's going, but just be careful you don't get flattened on the way

- Turquoise: Sea-lover, so not for someone who wants a stay-at-home partner, but very romantic

- Dark blue: Steady and safe, but not adventurous

- Mauve/blue: Has psychic ability, so there will be no hiding your innermost thoughts and desires

- Orange: Strong and courageous, liable to succeed where others fail – not a stay-at-home type

- Toffee: A career chaser, and can be ruthless, but will be a good provider

- Beige: Has problems but is improving

- Chocolate: An environmentalist who will spend most of their time saving whales, so if you are 'high maintenance' you might not be well-suited

- Rust: A hard worker/provider – can be a bit over-humble, and can turn into a doormat

- Terracotta: Rebel with or without a cause. You say black, he or she will say white, but will be fun with never a dull moment

- Gold: Sincere and honest, highly evolved spiritually, but maybe a little staid

- Pale green: Spiritually advanced, but still a learner, so apt to be confused and need long heart-to-heart discussions

- Mid-green: Able to heal you and willing to do so, no matter how many times you need it, but can be boring if you're a party animal

- Bright grass green: Friendly, gregarious. This means life and soul of the party, but not so good one-to-one

- Dark green: Can be mean, but thrifty, which is useful if you are always spending out of control

- Grey: Feels trapped and depressed and may pull you down

- Peach: Good talker/listener, but this means all the time – even when your favourite soap is on

- Pale pink: looking for true love, but inclined to soppy behaviour, so if someone showering you with roses at work might be an embarrassment, probably not one for you

- Bright pink: Happy in their career, but will insist that you need to be, too

- Violet: Has usually had a deep experience which has balanced and humbled him – a good mate, but not feisty in a fight

- Magenta: Entrepreneur, with fingers in every pie. Can have criminal tendencies if they're not controlled

- Bright red: Creative, but self-opinionated

- Rusty red: Argumentative and not willing to listen, but will be on your side in an argument, and will never quit

- Silver: Well connected to their angels, but a tendency to spend long hours in meditation

- Pearly: Medium abilities, so is inclined to bring spooky goings-on into your home

- Bright yellow: A dreamer – sweet, gentle and harmless, but not especially productive

- Pale yellow: Caring, empathetic and compassionate. This does mean, though, that if you're on your way to a party, they will insist on stopping for the injured toad and taking it to a rescue centre, no matter if you're wearing an Armani dress or a designer suit

Once you have learned to see the colours, they can be used in two ways. You could read your own colours (in a mirror) and go for someone with similar ones to you, which will give you a partner with similar ideas and plans. If you are both on the same level spiritually, the two of you will rarely disagree. But like to like doesn't always work, for instance if both of you have the colour of rusty red, then you will quarrel endlessly and never make up. Don't choose someone who is a depressive (grey) if you are, too, or things could get very downbeat round your place very quickly!

The alternative is to go for someone whose colours complement yours and fill in the gaps in your persona. For instance if you are often dreamy but not achieving much (bright yellow), go for a partner whose aura is orange (likely to succeed) or magenta (an entrepreneur) who might be able to help make your dreams come true!

Of course you may well see several strong colours in one person. If that's the case, then for this exercise you should concentrate on the heart area and the colour around it. This is the area that deals with perceptions and feelings regarding other people, so this is the one that will interest you most when looking for someone to have a loving relationship with. With auras, people have no choice but to show their *true colours!*

If all this is too much for you, then another possible way is to study the clothes of a person you like for a few weeks, always tuning in to your angel for guidance, until you develop a pattern of his or her colour choices, concentrating on the heart area – so shirts, sweaters and jackets. You will be able to build up a picture of the person's general preferences and then compare them to yours. These colours will almost always be reflected in the person's aura. Take a careful note of the colours you feel good in, to determine your own 'range'. Then use a decorator's colour-wheel to see which colours you clash with, which you match and which you are different from, but complement. Obviously if you clash, then steer clear, for no matter how gorgeous the person is, he or she will let you down in the end.

Once you've found your soul mate, don't forget to thank your angels for their help.

You could, of course, get an aura photo of the person done, but be aware that if you do this all aura photo-readers interpret the photos according to the charts provided with their particular camera. What you'll see if you succeed with the methods described above are entirely natural auras, and their meanings can be quite different to those compiled by the producer of an aura camera.

Whichever method suits you best, be sure and connect with your angels before you start, through clearing your mind and asking them in, and asking them for their guidance.

CHAPTER 9
ANIMAL ANGELS

Sometimes angels have four legs and whiskers.
– **Jenny Smedley**

Some animals shine with a perfect, pure light, sometimes just for a moment, sometimes for years or all their lives, and in doing so they bring their owners special joy or save them from danger, or help them with disability or make their lives more whole again after tragedy. These animals are filled with divinity, and their special stories deserve to be told.

Animals are the perfect host for angels because they are much more spiritual than we are a lot of the time. We are inherently Machiavellian, born to manipulate and use others to get our own way. We all lie, even if only little white lies that don't seem to do any harm. Our souls are sullied. However, animals are different. Animals love with a pure heart. People say that what we think of as unconditional love from our pets is actually just their survival instinct kicking in. In other words, they want to stay in our 'good books', as they need to be part of the pack in order to survive. I don't believe this is the case at all, and I'd counter by asking, so what is love, then?

- Love is being willing to make sacrifices for the happiness of someone else.

- Love is respecting someone else.

- Love is being willing to defend and protect someone else, sometimes putting ourselves at physical and emotional risk.

- Love is sharing.

- Love is trust.

- Love is loyalty.

Pets are in possession of all these loving attributes, therefore they do feel love.

This is illustrated by the story of Panda, the black-and-white mongrel.

Panda was never allowed upstairs in the house, although he was a much-loved member of the family. One night when he was 14 years old, the mother of this family, Pauline, woke to find him staring mournfully at her from the side of the bed. She was surprised because in all his 14 years Panda had never before broken this rule. She woke her husband, Colin, and they both stared at the dog. Panda turned and walked away but he didn't go downstairs. Instead Pauline and Colin, curious, followed him to their son Christian's bedroom, where Panda nudged the boy until he, too, woke up. The same thing happened with their 7-year-old daughter, Sophie. In a solemn line the family followed Panda down the stairs and into the kitchen, where the dog climbed wearily into his basket and closed his eyes. Within a few seconds Panda had stopped breathing and had passed away.

The only explanation for this behaviour is that Panda came upstairs to say goodbye to his family one by one. No creature who didn't know love and wasn't watched over by angels would have even thought of doing such a thing.

My dog, KC, is the reincarnation of my old dog, Ace. Ace showed her angelic side many times throughout her life, even saving my life. When KC was born she carried the omission of a missing nipple, the same one that Ace had lost during surgery a couple of years before she died. Recently another physical phenomenon has arrived as further evidence of Ace's rebirth as KC. Ace had scars. As a puppy, before we ever knew of her, she'd been scalded with boiling water. The resulting abscesses had left bald patches on her skin, on her upper right leg and part of her chest. In the past few months KC, who is a totally black dog, has started sprouting white hairs. These hair patches correspond exactly with the scars that Ace bore.

Angie sent me this story of a cat called Pudding:

'My granddad always used to tell us he would come back as a cat when he died, and we'd all smile and laugh and think nothing more of it. Then, when granddad died suddenly in his early sixties, it came as a dreadful shock to us all. I was only 8 at the time, and apart from losing a rabbit or a

guinea pig, this was my first "proper" experience of death.

'It was a few months later that a cat appeared in my Nanna's garden and adopted her. This beautiful long-haired tortoiseshell was called Fluffy, and Nanna was for-ever telling us this was Granddad come back. There were plenty of other cats that came into the garden, but none stayed like Fluff. Nanna had that cat for years before it sadly passed away.

'Now we jump to the mid-1990s. I have always adored Persian cats. I know they are bred very cruelly to make them look the way they do, and would never consider buying one from a breeder for that reason. Rescuing one, however, is a totally different story. Again, in Nanna's back garden a cat appeared. Because she'd had so many cats come and go, I thought nothing of it and didn't actually see it until the day someone said the magic word … Persian! I was round there like a shot, having decided no matter what, this cat was coming home with me! I went with my sister to Nan-na's, and there in an old ramshackle chicken shed, huddled tightly in a corner, with the biggest orange amber eyes you've ever seen, was this poor tatty cat, looking petrified. My sister pulled her from her hiding place and placed her in the cat carrier I was holding, and we promptly took her home.

'Once home, I opened the carrier and let her survey her new surroundings, and she had us all in hysterics when she made her way to a large potted plant on the floor because she needed to wee! From that day on, though, there was no doubt in anyone's mind whose cat she was, because she rarely left my side. I called her Pudding. The moment I got in from work, Pud met me at the front door, even knowing the sound of my car when I pulled up outside. She always wanted cuddles or a lap, and it had to be me if I was in. Other people were only good enough if I wasn't in.

'In 1997 she got a new little friend. Little did I know how close they would become, and how their friendship would blossom, but these two became real soul mates. Chester was a long-haired Peruvian guinea pig who had health problems, and he went blind within a year as a result, but he knew how to play and live! The two of them adored each other and would sit together, and sometimes Pud would pinch Chester's dried food when I wasn't paying attention. But sadly Chester died in January 2000, and Pudding never really got over losing him. I did get some more guinea pigs after him, but she never took to them at all. They weren't like he was and she simply didn't want to know.

'It was in the May of 2000 that I discovered that Pud had kidney cancer. I was absolutely beside myself. I noticed she'd not been well and her behaviour had changed in that she was distancing herself from me. It was as though she was preparing me for the parting that was shortly to follow. The vet said we could prolong her life by giving her injections once every three weeks, but by the second one it was obvious she'd had enough. So, cuddling up together, it was as though we decided together, somehow, that next time she went it wouldn't be a life-prolonging injection she would have but a final one, the one to let her go and be in peace.

'Those last days went way too quickly and I was a total wreck the night I took her and said goodbye. She passed away peacefully on my lap, and the sense, almost of euphoria, of peace and knowing I had done the right thing by her, was overwhelming. But there was one last strange thing she had to show me before she finally left. When I got home I showed her to my family before she was laid to rest next to her beloved Chester in the garden. I went into the kitchen and opened the back door, and as I did so, I saw my beautiful little Pudding run out past me and into the back garden she had loved so much, so I knew she was free and happy and out of pain.

'I believe Granddad came back twice as a cat, once for my Nanna and once for me. I have a photo of Pudding following one of Granddad's favourite habits ... reading the paper! She was a beautiful, playful and most loving animal, and I didn't have her with me long enough, but I will never ever forget her or the friendship we had. She was a very special little lady and I miss her so much. 14th July 2000 was her last day with us but I know she is happy where she is now, and when it's my turn to leave this mortal coil, the first face I want to see meet me is hers and little Chester pig's.

'Hope this hasn't made you cry like it has me! I didn't expect to be quite so emotional recalling all this, but looking at her photos, thinking about her and remembering those last days really has brought so much back. We have six cats now, and we love them dearly, but even my little Ruby, who *is my pride and joy and whom I love to pieces, will never recreate the experience and the special bond that Pudding and I had from day one.*

'After both Pud and Chester had died I had a film developed from an old camera. I don't recall taking the photo which I discovered and which almost had me in tears in the shop where I had them developed, but there in front of me was the most beautiful photo of Chester and Pudding lying side by side. I think it was their little gift to me.'

There are many stories such as this one. Why would a person think that a loved one came back as a pet? Is it possible? I think it has happened, and I also think that sometimes a pet is prompted by an angel to come and be with a certain person. And there's something incredibly special about these animals, some kind of angelic energy that's enough to bring solace to grief.

This is Gillian's story of another possible pet reincarnation:

'I was working at a dog shelter when on one particular occasion a very old and unhappy looking Jack Russell was sharing his run with the puppies. It was very cold and windy in the puppy pen and the dog had a snuffly, runny nose, and was wearing a jacket to keep him warm. He kept disappearing and hiding behind the bushes, and he looked so thoroughly miserable that my heart went out to him. After quite a bit of thought I decided to take him home

with me. The name the animal shelter had given him was Mr Grumpy.

'I'll never forget the soulful look he gave me as he was driven to my house. He had huge eyes with great depth to them. He was a bit on the stocky side and got his name because if any attempt was made to pick him up he would growl fiercely and look as though he was going to bite, even though he didn't have many teeth.

'Early in his stay with me I decided to give him a bone, and he immediately got it stuck on one of his remaining back teeth. The vet who removed it thought that Mr Grumpy was wrongly named and that, going by the state of his teeth, he'd probably never had a bone before in his life. I decided to rename him Tenby, which seemed to suit him.

'His growling was quite fearsome, so when we had occasion to get him into the car, we devised a method of coaxing him onto a blanket and then hoisting him, blanket and all, onto the back seat.

'He'd been living with me for about six months, and seemed to be settling in, when I went on holiday and left him in the care of a friend, who managed to lose him. I was heartbroken and scoured the district looking for him, asking all the neighbours and contacting the local animal shelters, but he was never found.

'Around this time, in my daily meditation, I attempted to tune in with him mentally and I asked him to show me where he was, so that I could find him and bring him home. As I asked the question my candle blew out, though *there was no wind or draft or movement of any kind in the room. I couldn't accept it then, but later I came to acknowledge that this was a communication from Tenby, telling me that he had moved into spirit.*

'Three or four months after this event, as I was driving along, very near to the spot where he'd gone missing, I saw a kitten at the edge of the road. I stopped the car and picked her up. She was bleeding from a gaping head wound, so I rushed her to the vet to get her stitched up. I was delighted to see that her colouring was ginger, black and white. She and I became very close and I called her Sparkles because she washed herself so much.

'It's my theory that Tenby reincarnated as the injured kitten to be with me again. The timing was just right, and who is to say whether this is possible, or true or not? Whatever the case may be, it made me so much happier to believe that Tenby had returned to me as Sparkles, and the hole in my heart was healed by her presence in my life.'

James sent me this wonderful story of how incredible the bond between pet and human can be, and also how some pets are imbued with a grace that belies their status as 'just animals':

'Pamela and I have been married for over 28 years and have always had beardies (bearded collies) as pets. In fact, our first one was actually a wedding present requested by Pamela. She had actually asked for a wolfhound, but I

thought it would be too big and too much work to look after, so I compromised when she came up with the idea of a beardie (I thought they'd be easy to look after. I know, I was young and innocent and knew nothing about the breed!).

'Anyway I'll skip on through the happy, happy years, to very recently. We currently have beardies numbers 4, 5 and 6: Star, who'll be 11 in November, Amy, who'll be 5 this week, as I write, and Fliss, who was 1 back in February.

'My darling Pamela had a stroke on 12th July 2009. It was a massive bleed and my sister-in-law and I spent an entire week camped up in the hospital by her bedside, willing her to pull through. The girls (our dogs) would spend the daytime in our car in the hospital car park. I would regularly get them out for a walk, and as soon as I had gotten them out of the car Star and Fliss would try and drag me off for a walk anywhere; however, Amy would pull me towards the hospital. She obviously knew "Mum" was somewhere in there and wanted to go and see her. This happened several times.

'It got to a point five days after Pamela was admitted that the doctor pulled me aside and regrettably asked me to face up to the fact that Pamela was not going to regain consciousness, and so we had to decide whether or not to go on to palliative care. I knew that Pamela had never wanted to be a vegetable in a bed, so over the course of the next few days the nurses and doctors made her as comfortable as possible so that she could slip away in peace and dignity. Vivienne (my sister-in-law) and I were convinced that she would slip away on Sunday 19th July, as the 19th is a significant date in both our families, being both Pamela's birthday and my own, also her older brother's, my parents' wedding anniversary, and the date Pamela's dad died. But she didn't.

'On the Monday the charge nurse for the ward came back after being off for the weekend, and asked how we were doing. We relayed the story and she asked if Pamela could be hanging on to see anybody. We couldn't think who. We had also mentioned the story about Amy trying to get into the hospital. Shyvonne, the nurse, immediately said maybe Pamela was waiting to see at least one of her girls, so we should go ahead and bring the dog in. A good friend who was looking after our girls during the night brought Amy in on the Monday afternoon for about an hour. Amy was as good as gold, just enjoying being next to her "Mum". Pamela sadly died that evening. So I'm convinced that Pamela was indeed not going to go without seeing Amy. Although we're very careful about not playing favourites, Amy is very special. She's so sensitive.

'When I'm having one of my meltdown moments at the loss of my beloved wife, Star and Fliss will come and sniff me, knowing something's wrong, but Amy keeps her distance for a while until they move off, and then after a few minutes she'll climb on board my lap and give the most therapeutic cuddle imaginable.'

James also told me that Pamela's older sister had bought my book, *Pets Have Souls Too*, for his wife, but she never got to read it. However, he did manage to read the first half-dozen pages to her whilst she was unconscious in the hospital, including a great favourite of theirs, 'Rainbow Bridge'. When it came time for him to tell her it was all right for her to go, he told her that she was on her way to meet up with their first three beardies (Sylvie, Katie and Heather), and that for a while they'd be looking after three of their girls each. It's wonderful that Amy still looks after James for Pamela, and brings him a little consolation.

Wendy sent me this beautiful tale:

'My best friend Lesley lost her father four years ago. She was very close to him and she misses him very much. He was a sheep farmer who kept many collies over the years, and they were all much loved. Just recently, Lesley has been having a very hard time at work and is completely exhausted. When she got her rota for work on Saturday she was very upset to see she had yet another week of gruelling shifts, and she felt like she was at the end of her tether. On Saturday night, she asked her Dad what she should do. She asked him to send her some help.

'The next morning (Father's Day), she got out of bed late and noticed a collie sitting on her driveway. She went out and the dog came over to her and brushed himself against her legs affectionately. He was a well-cared for dog and had a collar with a phone number on, so she went into the house and phoned the owner. While she did this, the dog sat at her feet and laid his head on her lap, as if they were old friends.

'When Lesley's husband and her own dog returned from their walk, her husband said the dog had been there since the early hours when he'd gone out, just sitting on the driveway as if he were waiting for someone. Lesley's dog, Nipper, and the collie were totally at home with each other, and Nipper never seemed to think it odd to have this strange dog in his house.

'Lesley is sure the dog came from her dad. She felt better for having him around and, on the Monday, feeling much stronger because of it, she went into work and sorted out her rotas once and for all.'

This story comes from Heila:

'I brought Rosie, my horse, from a dealer when she was about 12 years old. She was on the thin side with a bad cold, but we soon got her restored to fitness. She was such a beautiful girl, she was a cob/connemara cross, 14.1 hands high, and she had a teardrop-shaped birthmark on her hindquarters. I loved her so much, she really looked after me and I trusted her 100 per cent. We used to go out together with no saddle or bridle, just bareback and rope halter. When she cantered, if she felt I was unsafe she used to slow right down til I got my balance again. We truly bonded and loved each other. If she wanted anything she used to tell me by nudging me with her head, and she used to draw me into her chest and cuddle me.

'When Rosie was about 19, she developed cancer of the intestines. It was very quick, and within a week I knew what I had to do. It was the most heartbreaking decision I *have ever had to make, but the day I called the vet, before he arrived, she kept nudging me as if to say, "Come on, you know what you have to do." I worked at that time in a New Age shop, and there were mediums and psychics that used to work there, too. I too am very psychic and within a month I knew my Rosie hadn't left me, not really. I could "see" her and smell her and I could feel her with me when I was out walking my dogs. I told one of the mediums, and she said, "Next time you feel her around you, ask her if she'll allow you to step into her spirit." I did that, and oh what a wonderful experience it was! I immediately felt the bond again, which I'd thought was gone. It made me cry, but tears of joy.*

'It's now been about six years since Rosie passed over, but to this day she's still around me when I need her.'

Eleanor sent me this lovely tale:

'After losing our last puppy, Coco, who by then was 15½ years old, and had been our very first long-haired mini dachshund, my hubby and I were quite lonely and sad. We'd gone from having three mini dachshunds to losing all three in three years, and the house was of course very empty. 'It had been a few months since Coco had passed, and my hubby and I were in the basement doing some chores. We started talking about how much we missed Coco and how much we really loved her. We both fell silent for a minute and then we heard a strange noise from upstairs. There was a sound of a small ball being dropped and bouncing three

or four times (kind of like the sound of a ping pong ball).
'We both looked at each other in puzzlement. I'd certainly
never heard that noise before, and I'd spent many hours
in that basement. I went dashing upstairs to the area the
sound had come from. Of course I could find nothing, and
also realized that the floor is carpeted so we couldn't possi-
bly have heard a normal ball bouncing, but the sound had
been so unmistakeable.

'Suddenly I knew the answer and said to my husband,
"You realize that was Coco, letting us know she was still
with us in spirit?" Speaking with my daughter Alicia about
it later, she reminded me that when Coco was a young dog
she loved to play with a small rubber ball my daughter would
bounce for Coco to try and catch. I'd forgotten all about that.

'I also realized after talking to someone who had to put
their old dog to sleep and had wondered what to do with
the ashes, that I had all three dogs' ashes together in a desk,
right about where the bouncing ball noise had come from.
Upon further research I learned that the ping pong ball
bouncing is a paranormal phenomenon that others have
experienced. I have goose bumps and feel such a blessing to
have had that experience. Thanks Coco, for being our dog.'

Susan gave me this story of her animal angel:

'We got Dillan when he was 8 months old. My son rang me
from Exmouth and asked me if I wanted a labrador pup.
Of course I said yes, as I had recently lost my old girl who

was 17. I also had a small Jack Russell terrier, who was still lively, and I thought we still had room for another, as dogs are our lives.

'When Dillan came to us he was like a greyhound, frightened of everything and very aggressive towards dogs and people because he hadn't been socialized, but we loved him. It took us two years of hard work to bring out the qualities that made him so special. We took him on holidays and everywhere with us, when our Jack Russell grew really old (he was an incredible 21, in fact), we got a new terrier pup called Cindy. She loved Dillan with all her heart, and seemed to think he was her pup, even though he was 8 stone and she was not even 2! He had a really good life. Cindy cleaned him every morning, his ears, teeth and eyes. My God, she loved every inch of him. When he started to become poorly, and we took him to our vet, she diagnosed diabetes. I cried a lot, but even though I was scared stiff of needles I injected him every day, and he was OK, but then he started to have a job getting up because his back legs were giving out. He was strong; we knew that because he had got over a stroke and he had had his spleen removed, but still he battled on.

'One evening I went to work and had only been gone ten minutes when my phone rang. It was my husband telling me that Dillan's legs had gone again, and this time we knew what we had to do. It was the hardest thing ever, as he was fine from the waist up, but our vets were brilliant. We found it the hardest thing in the world, our best friend had gone, and the house was empty.

'We were devastated. It will be four years next March, and it still hurts. Cindy grieved more than us. We fostered several labs, but she didn't accept any, until Gus came along. He was another black lab from lab rescue. He looked like Dillan, and is very respectful towards her. She loves him, although he's scared stiff of her.

'He's really naughty on the lead, although perfect in every other way. When we were on holiday I kept saying I was going to swap him for a black poodle as a joke. Cindy was running around chasing him, but she doesn't play with other dogs (she's a proper lady); only plays with her mates who live nearby. 'We went to Cockington near Torquay, and a black poodle there made a bee-line for Cindy, although there were hundreds of other dogs around. Her tail was wagging like mad. I let her off and they ran around together like old mates. It was amazing how she just seemed to accept this poodle instantly. 'Then I got the real shivers and goose bumps because the owner came along and called the poodle by name: "Dillan!"

'You could have knocked us over with a feather. "I'm sorry, what did you call him?"

She said, "Dillan".

'I then asked how old he was, and she said, "He's three and a half."

'This was almost exactly the same length of time since we'd lost Dillan. I don't believe in lots of things, but I believe that was our Dillan, and that Cindy knew it.'

Rachel gave me this story, which I have to say, is one of my all-time favourites:

'This story is actually one that happened to my mother when my older brother was a baby (before I was born.) The year was 1976 and my mom and dad lived in Cumberland, Maryland. My brother was a small baby. My dad taught art classes at the nearby college in Frostburg, and my mother was a stay-at-home mom. They would often attend small parties with some of my father's colleagues that would last late into the night. My mom was not much of a party type, but she would sometimes come along and bring my brother with her to these get-togethers.

'One of these nights, my mom decided to leave and walk home. My father did not want to leave yet, so he stayed behind. My mother started out up the long street, which was on a steep hill, pushing my brother in a stroller. It was late and the town was somewhat quiet, with few cars passing by. A few minutes into the walk, she passed a man on the opposite side of the street. As she glanced over at him, she realized the man was exposing himself to her. Gripped with fear, she walked faster, scared for her infant son and herself. She was now too far from the party to turn back but still a while yet from the house.

'With chills, she realized that the creep had crossed the road and was following her. He began to shout things at her. She upped her walking speed, but the man still followed.

'Then out of nowhere, two large dogs appeared from be-tween the rows of houses. They walked next to her, some-what playfully nipping at each other. They never asked for her attention, just walked next to her, circling around her as she pushed my brother. From that point, and for at least the next 15 minutes, she walked with the dogs forming al-most what seemed like a circle of protection around her and her baby.

'The creep persisted in trailing her for several minutes, and shouted a few times, "Those your dogs, miss? Those your dogs?" but eventually he fell back and walked away. Even in his seemingly drunk state, he knew not to mess with someone who was flanked by two big dogs!

'As she turned the last corner to get home, the dogs walked off the other way, fully present, and then just like that, they weren't there. They'd appeared and stayed with her the entire time she needed them, and then faded off like mist when she got to the safety of her own street. She has always thought of them as guardian angels for her and my baby brother, and I believe they were!'

I've always said that angels can appear to you either just as you expect them to look or just as they need to look. I have no doubt in my mind that these two 'dogs' were a lot more than they appeared.

It's not just mammals who have angels in their souls. Matt sent me this wonderful tale of two crows.

'We live in the country, right out in the middle of nowhere, and are quite used to all sorts of wild animals around us, and their behaviour. But recently we started to notice that the crows that had set up a nest in our chimney for the summer were acting really strange. They would sit on my car bonnet and peck at the windscreen, really hard, too, so that you can still see the chips on the glass! I'd wake up every morning to this really loud pecking and open the window of my bedroom to scare them off. They were doing this for maybe about a week and I could think of nothing to stop them. They started to do the same thing to the landing window and we thought that maybe it was because in between the double glazing was some sort of silver strip around the outside of the window and I heard somewhere they liked shiny things.

'We tried everything, from covering the windows with mustard to hopefully put them off the idea, to putting a big stuffed toy cat in the window to act as a scarecrow. Nothing worked. We didn't know what to do and in the end just had to live with it.

Our big German shepherd dog then began to act a little funny and would look at our fireplace and tilt his head to one side as if he had heard something stuck in the chimney. My mum came to me saying she thought a bird was trapped in the chimney, so we went to investigate. With a torch we looked up the chimney as far as we could, and lo and behold there was not one but two little baby crows that had fallen from the nest nearly into the fireplace.

'It took me a while to reach up the chimney as far as I could (it's a really small fireplace and not much room to reach up) and, one at a time, manage to catch the baby crows.

'We carefully checked over them and it looked like they had been there for days. They were really scraggy looking, covered in soot and so skinny and worn out they couldn't even cry for their mum.

'We gave them some bread and water and sat with them for a while until they regained some energy, and after a couple of hours one of them started to call for his mum. She would circle us overhead, keeping a keen eye on her young, so we left them both outside on our garden table for the mum to come to them. One of the babies had obviously learned to fly, and after a while we saw him take off and fly over our house and away. The other one, however, was in a bad state, it was so weak and helpless it couldn't do anything but call out for its mum with the small voice it had. We left the baby in our outside chicken run with some shelter from a wooden box filled with straw and some food and water, this way if the mum wanted to come to the baby she could. As we were caring for her young she and the dad would circle us overhead and sit in the trees watching, and I believe without a doubt that they knew what we were doing.

'Sadly the weak baby had died by the next morning so we put him under a nearby tree so his mum could find him.

'After reading your book Pets Have Souls Too, I put two and two together and realized that the parents pecking our *windows every day was them trying to tell us about the plight of their young.*

'I've heard that animals do not have the concept skills we have and if you were to, for example, drop a ball on a table a dog would look for it on the floor as it doesn't understand the concept of higher surfaces, but I totally disagree and I now know that the parent crows knew exactly what had happened to their young and that they were inside our house!

'This is another example of how man and animal can communicate in a way, and could have possibly been great friends had man not driven fear into every living animal on our planet.'

I totally agree with Matt there, and I feel that a love and respect for animals is the answer to halting humanity's spiral into spiritual decay.

Sally sent me this story of a cat that seemed, for just one moment, to have angelic power:

'I always say that there is a reason for everything, so when my beloved cat, Christa, was run over and killed, I tried to tell myself that there was a reason for that, too. Christa was crossing a road that she'd crossed safely hundreds of times, but this time she was hit. We never knew who did it because we didn't find her for several hours. Christa and I were very close and she always used to come when I called her. She used to lay across my shoulders while I walked around our garden.

'Two months after she died I was driving home. I was nearing a rather nasty crossroads, not far from where Christa had been killed. Naturally I always thought of her whenever I passed that place, and this day it was the same. As I neared the fatal spot, I could make out a small shape on the road. I braked frantically, and as I got nearer I could make out that it was a cat crouching there. It was the same colour as Christa, but I told myself there are thousands of tortoiseshell cats around. It couldn't be her! The car wasn't slowing quickly enough, and I started to panic, as the cat didn't look like it was going to move. I couldn't bear the thought that I was going to kill another cat, right where Christa had died. "No!" I screamed, "Move!"*

'The cat stood up. Shivers ran over my body as I could see that it was Christa! "Christa!" I cried. She didn't move, and the car slid irresistibly towards her, turning sideways as it went. It was like one of those nightmares: the car seemed to be moving in slow motion, but no matter how hard I stood on the brakes it wasn't going to stop in time. Why didn't she move? I asked myself. The cat's face stared at me over the bonnet of the car, and even though I knew it wasn't possible, there is no doubt it was Christa looking back at me. The car loomed over her and there was a sickening thump, followed by a bump as a tyre went over her.*

'Finally the car slewed to a stop, sideways across the road. At that very second there was an ear-splitting hooting and a roaring sound, as an oil tanker shot across the crossroads without even slowing down. It was in my right-of-way,* *and if I hadn't stopped where I had, the tanker would have ploughed into my car. I found out later that the tanker had failed to stop because of a hydraulic brake failure.*

'I stood looking after the tanker for a moment, and then thought of the cat that had saved my life. I rushed along the car to the back and looked. There was nothing: no blood, no fur, no torn body. There was not a sign of a cat anywhere.'

It might seem like all these experiences only come with fluffy or feathered cute animals, but that isn't always the case. In my recent reading for Jade Goody's mum, Jackiey Budden, Jade told me to tell her mum about a little pale yellow butterfly that she was using to watch over her. Jackiey confirmed that indeed a little yellow butterfly had been following her around, all over the world, for months.

Lastly, Tony Byford of the SOS Animal Rescue in Spain sent me this lovely story of one of his own dogs. People like Tony have my upmost respect, as they help animals in highly emotional, tough circumstances, and I'm not sure I'd have the courage to face what they face.

'I share my house with my friend Jose, who is clairvoyant, and we obviously have dogs and cats sharing the house, too. Last Friday one of the dogs, Popeye, was not very well and didn't want to go out or eat. He was 12 years old, so we put him in his bed in a room quietly by himself, checking up on him frequently. On Saturday morning I asked Jose if he'd been in to Popeye, and he told me yes, he had, but that very

sadly Popeye had died. Jose then went on to tell me that he'd already known Popeye had gone because during that Friday night, whilst half asleep, he'd had the sensation of a dog lying on the bed with him, and a man in a white cape or tunic sitting in the chair beside the bed. He also spoke of a sensation of the dog that was lying on him rising up, making the mattress and Jose himself move as well. When he woke up, he went into the room where Popeye was and found he had passed on. Jose has no idea who the man was, but only remembers this white cape. Popeye had been with us since he was a puppy, and in fact we still have his mother. We'll be getting his ashes back this week, and we'll bury them in the garden.'

Tony asked me what this might mean. I felt that because of the wonderful work they do, they obviously have a beautiful connection to animals, dogs in particular. To me this was a clear sign from the spirit world that their work is looked upon with grace. I believe the being was one of the animals' angels showing itself, to prove that animals are every bit as entitled to have angels as humans are.

At this point I'd like to mention a woman called Margaret Barker. She is elderly and frail now, but she spent most of her life trying to get the role of animals in war recognized. She once rescued an old warhorse called Joey, one of the few to be returned alive to British shores. Being an avid reader and hungry for information about history, Margaret recalls finding a book with graphic details of the First World War, amongst which were pictures of animals sent to the front. These images were imprinted on Margaret's mind, as she became aware of the sacrifice paid by all concerned. She never forgot the price Joey and millions like him paid.

It was about this time that Margaret came to believe that animals should be commemorated on Remembrance Day alongside the soldiers they'd worked for and died with. Recently Margaret's wishes have started to come true, and I was one of many around the country who laid a special wreath on Memorial Day to commemorate those horses, dogs, cats and pigeons who died under fire. This is in no way to detract from the people who died, but I'm sure that any one of them, if asked, would be only too pleased to have their animal brethren remembered and honoured.

Man has always dragged animals, who are innocent and unknowing, into the fields of fire. My heart breaks, particularly for the horses. To see depictions of those noble creatures galloping towards guns breaks my heart. They have no conscious knowledge of the concept of war, of killing or of dying. They have no understanding of what the gunfire or the flashing lights mean, and when they find themselves lying, dying on the cold ground, the fear they feel must be indescribable. Wikipedia carries these sobering facts, among others, concerning dogs in warfare:

Approximately 5,000 US war dogs served in the Vietnam War. About 10,000 US servicemen served as dog-handlers during the war, and the K9 units are estimated to have saved over 10,000 human lives. 43 military working dogs and 73 US servicemen working as dog-handlers were killed in action during the war. US military regulations required destruction or transfer of military working dogs in combat zones, and no known Vietnam war dogs returned home.

It makes it all the more strange and unjust that there are still people in the world who treat animals with indifference, as if they were no more than machines. I'm totally sure that anyone who has had an animal beside him in a time of fear or conflict would agree that, indeed, some angels have four legs.

It seems fitting that the last word about animals should go to a military man, and someone possibly not renowned for his connection to animals. This passage from Napoleon's memoirs tells of the depth of devotion animals have for us. When it was reported that 'A soldier's mastiff was sat with his dead owner trying to rouse him at the battle of Marengo in Italy. When all his efforts failed he tried to get Napoleon to come over to where his master lay, somehow believing that perhaps, of all men, he could do something', Napoleon wrote:

This soldier, I realized, must have had friends at home and in his regiment: yet he lay there where he fell, deserted by all except his dog. In the past and throughout my life I have looked on, unmoved at battles which decided the future of nations. Tearless, I had given orders which brought death to thousands. Yet here I was, stirred, profoundly stirred to tears, and by what? By the grief, loyalty and courage of one dog for his master.

CHAPTER 10
ANGEL VOICES, ORBS AND LIGHTS

We shall find peace. We shall hear the angels, and we shall see the sky sparkling with diamonds. – **Anton Chekov**

HOW CAN YOU RECORD AN ANGEL'S PRESENCE?

EVPs

One way to try and record an angel's presence is with what is called EVP – Electronic Voice Phenomena. Many people claim to have recorded the voices of spirits with this method, but some people believe they have captured the voice of their own guardian angel, too.

Don't forget, if you do manage to record the voice of your loved one, then it will have been enabled by their angel. Always meditate first, asking your angel to protect and guide you and, if it is their will, to allow you to record them. Make sure you do this first to prevent any negative energies from coming through.

The good thing about this kind of evidence is that if you manage to record some intelligible voices, and what they are saying makes some kind of sense, it's very good proof of the existence of another (i.e. angel/spirit) dimension. Clear voices can't be explained away as radio interference or other sound pollution if the experiment is done correctly.

How to Record an EVP

You'll obviously need some kind of recording device. This can be anything from a digital or tape recorder to a phone answer machine. Whichever machine you choose, try to make it one that has a counter, so that if you do record something you'll be able to find it afterwards. There's nothing more frustrating than picking up something and then being unable to locate it on the tape later.

Another good idea is to use a machine with a remote microphone rather than one that's built into the machine, because the latter can pick up the noise from the machine, which could mask or pollute the voice you're trying to record. If the microphone has a long cord you can place it away from the machine and avoid this problem.

Test the machine before you start so that you know the kind of background noise to expect. Obviously place the machine away from any other noise sources such as air-conditioners, ventilators, refrigerators – even fish tanks, as the hum of the filters can ruin an EVP.

It's a good idea always to start with a fresh tape, as even if you think you've recorded fully over something else with your EVP, some noise can bleed through.

Now, when you're ready, put the recording volume up to its highest level and ask your angels to allow your loved one to come through to you. After this, try not to move, as even clothes rustling can spoil the clarity of your EVP. If you want to you can even leave the room at this point and just leave the tape running, because it's unlikely that you'll hear anything with your ears.

Once you come to listen to the tape it's better to use headphones, as this will make it easier to hear any possible EVP and also cut down on any outside noise. You may only get one or two words at your first attempt, but you'll soon, with experience, be able to distinguish voices from the background noise. Once you do start to get words that you can hear from your loved one or angel, write them all down, because the first ones you get are unlikely to make sense at first. After a while, though, they should do.

ORB AND ANGEL LIGHT PHOTOGRAPHY

A lot of people think that orbs and angel lights are recent phenomena, and blame their appearance on digital cameras, but in fact I've been sent images of orbs and lights that have appeared in old, sometimes even black-and-white photos from decades before the invention of digital cameras. People come up with all kinds of explanations for these odd 'captures'. Some say they are simply light anomalies, damp droplets or dust. Some people think they are bubbles of ectoplasm, some that they are electromagnetic energy. Some people think they are 'leakages' from another dimension, and some that they are manifestations of aliens from another world. They could be any of these things. They could also be evidence of a passed-over loved one, or an angelic presence.

If you want to capture some genuine spirit orbs and have no idea where or when to start, a good tip is to keep an eye on your pets. Dogs and cats in particular seem to be able to see orbs with their naked eye, and will often try to play with them. To us our pets just look as if they're playing with something invisible, of course. Take some photos if you catch your pet doing this, and see what you get.

As I've said before, people are very quick to label orbs as light anomalies, but angels will sometimes still use these if it helps them get through. In these cases it very much depends on the circumstances at the time the orbs appear: if you've been asking for a sign and orbs suddenly start popping up in your photos, then you have your answer. But be aware that these signs will be simply for you personally, and won't necessarily convince anyone else that they are real spirit manifestations.

How to Capture Orbs

Of course you'll need a camera. Digital ones are best because you get instant results. You don't have to be very skilled at photography to capture orbs, although of course the more in focus everything is, the easier it is to interpret what you've got. To keep genuine results to a maximum and spurious ones to a minimum, don't take your photos where there are bound to be dust molecules or water droplets floating around. For this reason it's best to avoid photos taken at night outdoors, especially in somewhere like a cave, because in those instances you're more likely to get orbs than not, but they won't be in any way paranormal. Obviously avoid rain, as drops will form on the lens. Don't take photos directly into the sun, because the resulting light effects will also largely nullify your results. Don't walk about too much if you're outdoors, as this will kick up dust. Make sure your camera lens is free from fingerprints or greasy smudges of any kind, because though the results might at first look impressive and as if they're genuine objects captured in the photo, any close examination will soon reveal them for what they are.

Before you start shooting, state your intent to your angels in a meditation so that the energy around you is receptive to receiving a photographic sign.

HOW TO TELL IF ORBS AND LIGHTS ARE SPIRITS OR ANGELS

You can be pretty sure you've captured something interesting if:

- The orb on your photo appears to be moving fast. Dust and water molecules don't move fast enough to cause a blur.

- The orb is a strange shape. Dust and water have a classic routine shape. Anything that deviates from the norm is something unusual.

- The orbs are brightly coloured (usually red, orange or blue/mauve). Dust and water rarely show up with colours.

- There is just one orb in the photo. It's more likely to be a spirit sign if the photo is not crowded with them. Crowds of orbs are more likely to be dust or water clouds.

- The orb is clearly partially behind another object. Dust and water molecules will be on the lens, so they cannot move behind something in shot.

- The orb has a clear face on it – especially if the face can be identified!

- The orbs have a halo or are luminescent.

- The orb has six or eight sides, as this is the most likely shape for transcending different dimensions.

- The orbs are very bright white and have no dots inside them.

- The orbs are solid looking – often egg shaped rather than round.

- The orbs reflect light, as this proves they are three-dimensional and therefore a complete orb rather than a flat circle.

- The orb has a tail.

- It grows in progressive photos.

If you capture a light or mist rather than an orb, then it will be of interest if:

- There was nothing around to create the mist, such as a fire, someone smoking in the vicinity, or actual low cloud or mist.

- The light isn't round but has a shape to it, which can be cloud-like or can actually form the shape of a person, an angel or an object.

- The mist has a coloured halo.

- The light is coloured, but not symmetrical in shape.

- The coloured light shadows a person in the photograph, like an aura.

- The light is fast moving and has a tail, like a comet.

- It progresses across the scene in fast-frame photography.

- It grows in progressive photos.

Bear in mind that even an orb or misty shape that turns out to have been created by a light anomaly can still in fact also be an angel message. Angels will use whatever means are at their disposal!

CONCLUSION

He shall give his angels charge over thee, to keep thee: And in their hands they shall bear thee up, lest at any time thou dash thy foot against a stone. – **Luke 4:10-11**

I hope that perhaps by now you've come to see that angels aren't just around for the privileged few. It can be hard to stay positive when it seems that everything around you is going wrong, but with a bit of application you'll be able to make contact with the angels' realm and get your life back on track.

The best ways to do this are:

- Meditation – only by closing down all of your worries and concerns about everyday life will your energy become calm enough for angels to reach through to you. Meditation can also raise your own vibration and thereby bring you closer to them. There are many good CDs on the market that can help you, or, if you have trouble reaching a calm state on your own, why not join a circle to sit with other like-minded people? Group energy can often help if you're not able to reach the right state by yourself. You can get this help in mystical circles, where people are trying to heal each other or develop their own psychic abilities, or you can join a group that practises yoga or some sort of Buddhist meditation. It doesn't matter which path you choose, as they will all help.

- Visualization – just as if you were playing a DVD, picture the life you would like rolling through your mind in every detail. The more you can see every detail, and the more real you can make it, the more you're tapping into your own ability to change reality, and also preparing your mind to accept angelic help to make your life change for the better. So, see everything. If you're, for instance, focusing on moving to a new home, see everything about it: the colours, the doors, the windows, the garden, the furniture, the wall colours, the kitchen, every room. Walk around the house in your mind and make it real. Feel what it would be like to live there. Make it yours.

- Be positive. Like I've said, positive energy is tranquil energy, and if you're surrounded by it, it makes it much easier for you and your angels to connect and interact together. A focus picture, as described in *Angel Whispers*, is still the best tool I know to encourage positivity. Being positive won't make your path through life change in a second, but it will be the start of changing everything. Basically, to do this you create a focus for positive thoughts by drawing a picture that symbolizes how you would like your life to be, and writing an eight-word mantra around the image. By staring at this image every morning before you even get out of bed, and repeating the mantra several times, you'll set your day up to go positively, and lessen the impact of any negative events.

- Go for past-life regression with a hypnotherapist. This is the best way I know to start to reconnect with your own deep spirituality. By learning who you really are, by learning who you have really been, not only will you find yourself but you'll find your soul angel, and with this powerful being on your side there will be every chance you can change things in this life. If you think about it you'll no doubt realize that you've been surrounded by clues to your past life since you can remember. The signs can be subtle, like odd dreams or vision-like daydreams of other places and times, or an abiding interest in a certain era – perhaps the clothes suit your style and make you feel complete, or you like to collect artefacts from a certain time because they feel familiar and make you content. Or these clues can be more forceful, like unexplained phobias or obsessions that have no roots in your current life. Put the clues together and you can be sure that, when you're regressed, the past life you recall will fit with them. This is evidence of your soul angel at work.

- Take the path of least resistance. Sometimes we resist angelic help because we have no idea that's what we're fighting against. If it seems that 'bad luck' is dogging your every move, and no matter what efforts you make to advance, life just keeps shutting doors in your face, it can only really mean one thing: you are knocking on the wrong doors. Angels will try to 'herd' us towards our right destiny, even if it's not a direction we would have chosen consciously. Once we listen and allow ourselves to be herded, we have every chance of happiness. So, if this happens to you, sit back and think about it, and look for some alternative to your perceived route. It's probably staring you in the face. There is always a choice, and by taking the one that resists you least, you can be sure you've taken the right path. One word of warning, though: sometimes you are meant to fight for something. But the general rule seems to be that if you get knocked back or down three times, then you have to accept that you're being guided in another direction.

- Start small. If you think that your angel is ignoring you, or that you don't even have one,

you can bet that your angel is trying very hard
to convince you otherwise, but sometimes when
we're in the midst of 'being human' we just can't
or won't see it. So, start small. Ask for some small
sign, such as a feather in an unlikely place, or for
a certain song with certain lyrics to come on the
radio at a certain time. This is the really great
thing about angel communication – you can
always tell if you're making progress, because if
you are there will be signs of it. Look for anything
unusual, for angels are nothing if not inventive,
and they'll use all and any means you can possibly
imagine, and some you can't, to get through to
you. So, make a note of anything whatsoever
that's unusual, or stands out in your day. Once
you start to notice these things, their incidence
will increase and start to build up a picture. Don't
miss the signs or allow your left brain to talk you
out of them. The more you believe in angels,
the more you'll see signs of their presence, until
what's happening becomes irrefutable proof, to
you.

- Listen to the sort of music that calms you and
takes you out of yourself. Anything that distracts
and soothes the conscious mind will help you
connect with angels. Crystal bowls, Tibetan
singing bowls and gongs all have a part to play.
Sound therapy in any form can transform

your brain waves and make you receptive to communication from a higher realm.

- Connect with your inner child. This will take your mind-frame back to a time when angelic connection was natural. Do this by recalling a time when as a child you were sad or unhappy. Perhaps you'd displeased a parent and felt you were unfairly chastised. See yourself standing in front of your current self as a child. Accept that now you are the adult you have the power to comfort that child and make everything all right. Open your arms and welcome that child into your current self. Feel the light and innocence of the child transforming your current self, which may be negative and burdened with the responsibilities of adulthood, into the wondrous state of childhood. By healing that small trauma in your child self, you'll be able to bring your current self closer to the rapture of angels.

- Take time to stop and gaze at the beauty of the planet. Stand and stare at the best view you can find and allow your mind to be filled with love for the Earth and the universe itself. This is the way to manifest more beauty and protect the planet. Don't rush, take your time, and appreciate the wonders of animals and nature. Don't always be running in the rat race, because your spiritual wealth in the long run will be much greater and more important than material wealth. This is because you can take spiritual wealth with you.

- Make notes of any unusual dreams you have, especially if they happen just as you're going to sleep or just before you wake up. Keep a dream diary beside the bed; after a few months you'll be amazed at how the dreams translate into an ongoing message, or a cosmic jigsaw puzzle of how things should be. Trust the messages you receive.

- Use divination cards. They can be tarot or angel cards or really any sort that is aesthetically pleasing to you. With practice you can get angel messages this way, not so much with a literal translation of the meaning of the cards as written, but in ways that are meaningful to you personally.

- Try any and all angel therapies, because sometimes your angel will resort to communicating with you through a third party, an 'earth angel', as they're sometimes called. Apart from the obvious possible benefits, if you connect and interact with a therapist who is in the right place angelically, it will benefit your state of mind and state of being.

- If you're a victim of depression, try to understand that, sometimes, pushing us down into this state is the only way angels can open us up enough to hear them. I liken it to them treating us like one of those little plastic frogs with the sucker on the bottom. We get pushed down harder and harder until there's nowhere else to go (in other words we can think of nothing else and so the angel has been successful at shutting off our physical body's emotional responses to the mundane). Then we get released and shoot up into the air just like the frog when his sucker becomes unstuck. This was how it was for me, and the message I got at that moment really did change everything for me in a split second. If this is how you feel, allow yourself to begin to expect the release at any second. Know that you are being prepared for a new understanding and a new reality. Be ready to grab it when it appears. Nurture a growing sense of wonder and, the more you do that, the more it will grow, until one day you'll look back, as I do now, from a different place and a different world.

- Once you do feel that you're getting closer to your angels, don't forget to 'ask'. Angels can only intervene in our lives in ways we'd like them to if asked to do so. Don't be afraid to ask, because you are entitled to do so. Once you have asked, though, be patient. Heaven's time doesn't always run on schedule with ours. If events seem to you to be going off-track, don't despair. We can never imagine the route to our angel's goal. Looking back you'll see a map laid out that you followed, but when you're following the route some of it may not seem to make much sense. This is because angels have a very complicated task trying to help us without disrupting other people's lives.

- When things do happen, make sure you say 'thank you.' Although angels won't be offended if you don't, because they love you unconditionally, it doesn't hurt to be polite! The emotion of gratitude is also a positive emotion, so feeling that way will encourage the release of endorphins in your brain, also known as 'happiness chemicals'. The more of these that you produce on a regular basis, the more you're training your brain to be receptive to happiness. You'll literally build happiness receptors in your brain, and your way of being will naturally evolve in that direction.

- Be nice to people. This is another way of building positivity, but also angels have been known to appear in human guises. This isn't exactly a test, but it is a way for us to have an opportunity to express ourselves positively. So, if someone asks you a favour, especially a stranger, and you're able safely to help them, seriously consider doing so, because you never know who might be watching! You can also be partially responsible for other people's journey through their day, and the course it takes. Imagine waking up grumpy. You hear the doorbell and stub your toe rushing to answer it. You scrabble for the doorknob and tear your fingernail. Then you open the door and there stands the postman with nothing more than a big stack of junk mail. You yell at him for getting you out of bed, and he feels upset and belittled. He goes back to the sorting office and yells at the man on the parcel counter. This man clocks off, goes home in a bad mood and shouts at his wife for nothing. The wife feels sad and alone. Perhaps her angel was just getting through to her, and now it becomes impossible. A fanciful scenario, I suppose, but everything does have an equal and opposite reaction, so it could happen in a similar way to this. By your actions you will enable people to perceive angels in you, and this will help you in turn. Try to perceive angels in others, too. Pass it forward, as they say.

- Pass it forward, yes. This is a wonderful way to be. If you do someone a favour, and they offer to pay you – if you don't really need the money, tell them to 'pass it forward'. In other words, they too should do an unexpected favour for someone else. It's a way of changing the people of the world, one step at a time, and will surely help you on your quest to speak with angels.

- For your own benefit, stay away from habitually grumpy, negative people. It might sound harsh, but I recall once attending a wonderful meditation class on anger at a local Buddhist centre. After the session, which threw up some interesting angry thoughts I didn't know I had, I asked the monk in charge, 'What should I do if there's a specific person who always makes me angry, and even though I've tried to help them, things don't change?' He told me I should stay away from this person, because at the end of the day I had responsibility for my own spirit, and not theirs. They were damaging me, he said, and I owed it to myself not to allow that. So, even if the 'someone' is a family member – if you simply never get along, walk away, because you'll never be able to be positive around them, or change them.

- Don't read newspapers or watch the news unless you really need to. Bad news is what sells broadcasts and papers, sadly. The more you feed this kind of thing, whether it be doomsayers or war items, the stronger the concept grows.

We can't change the whole world to a positive place overnight, but if we refuse to nurture the negativity, then slowly but surely we will change the world for ourselves, and the more people who do that, the more the world itself will change. Be especially careful not to watch anything negative just before or during eating. It has been proved scientifically that negative emotions do affect the molecular structure of what we eat and drink. Saying grace over your food and injecting love into it will mean the food will then nourish your soul as well as your body.

- Stop criticizing yourself, for this puts you into a state of negativity. Forgive yourself for any mistakes you might make, and declare that today is the first day of the rest of your life. Draw a line under things you may have done or said that keep running over and over in your mind. Your angel will give you unconditional love, so long as you can give it to yourself. Likewise, don't criticize other people. Don't talk about fears and world issues, don't dwell on anything negative. People think there's nothing they can do about the problems the world faces, environmental and social. This isn't true, but they won't change the world's problems by granting these things more power or energy. The more something is fed by people thinking and talking about it, the more that reality is created and the more likely it is to manifest. Instead, focus on and talk about good things, about heart-warming acts of bravery, about miracles, no matter how small, about how great the world will be when we all get along and take care of it better. In this way you will become a 'light worker' and you'll join the ranks of those working to manifest a better reality for all of us. Don't talk to doomsayers, for they are working, albeit unknowingly, to manifest a worse reality for the world. Don't join them.

In conclusion, think about what you say and do and try to create within yourself a heaven where angels would not fear to tread, but would be welcomed. This is your right, and every single person can do it. Just believe. The more you see, hear and feel angels, by training yourself to do so, the more you'll become part of the angelic realm and the more they'll become part of your life, every single day.

BOOKS

Dear Angel Lady – Jacky Newcomb: www.jackynewcomb.com
Awoken by an Angel – Laurence Stanway: www.lulu.com/content/paperback-book/awoken-by-an-angel/870984
How to Hear Your Angels – Doreen Virtue
Drawing Angels – Mimi Doe

WEBSITES

Laura Lyn: www.angelreader.net
www.sos-animals.org
margretbarker.co.uk
www.chilling-tales.com
www.SpiritualParenting.com

PRODUCT INFORMATION

I advocate using silk for your angel sanctuaries in my books, but some silk involves what I consider to be animal cruelty. Get cruelty-free silk here: www.ahimsasilks.com

NOTES

NOTES

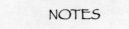

NOTES

NOTES